The Essential Guide to UFO Sightings Since 1945

Frank Schwede

4880 Lower Valley Road • Atglen, PA 19310

Copyright © 2017 by Frank Schwede

Library of Congress Control Number: 2017935732

Type set in ITC Avant Garde Gothic Std

ISBN: 978-0-7643-5437-3

Previous ISBN: 978-3-613-03720-5

originally copyrighted by Motorbuch Verlag, Postfach 10 37 43, 70032 Stuttgart. A company of the Paul Pietsch-Verlage GmbH & Co. KG [Ltd. Partnership] 1st Edition 2014

Printed in China

Published by Schiffer Publishing, Ltd.
4880 Lower Valley Road
Atglen, PA 19310
Phone: (610) 593-1777; Fax: (610) 593-2002
E-mail: Info@schifferbooks.com
Web: www.schifferbooks.com

For our complete selection of fine books on this and related subjects, please visit our website at www.schifferbooks.com. You may also write for a free catalog.

Schiffer Publishing's titles are available at special discounts for bulk purchases for sales promotions or premiums. Special editions, including personalized covers, corporate imprints, and excerpts, can be created in large quantities for special needs. For more information, contact the publisher.

We are always looking for people to write books on new and related subjects. If you have an idea for a book, please contact us at proposals@schifferbooks.com.

Contents

Preface

A reader might certainly be surprised that a serious publisher could come to publish a book about UFOs, which belong to the realm of pseudo-scientific knowledge and esoteric literature. So you inevitably have to ask the question: UFOs and reliability—do they really go together? The clear answer is: Yes. For one thing, at first, it was indeed true that the acronym UFO only stood for the term: "Unidentified Flying Object" or even "Unknown Flying Object." And yes, what is unknown is, to begin with, everything we could not identify at first glance (sometimes at second glance); that is, could not explain. It might be a big, faraway bird or a hot-air balloon, which, due to its distance, appears to remain stationary over one place for a long time—thus, definitely issues that initially have nothing to do with extraterrestrial life. Only after closer analysis of photos or film materials, which don't provide any conclusive explanation for the object they illustrate, does the area of speculation keep expanding and finally lets us come to the thesis that, in some cases, extraterrestrial visitors are involved.

Secondly, I want to attempt not to rule out any possibility in assessing unidentified objects—including extraterrestrial life. There are good reasons for this, and I will go into more detail in the individual chapters. It should be said beforehand that this book is not a scientific work, but a book that will appeal to a group of readers who may be dealing with this issue for the first time and more out of pure curiosity. I would like to present you with a small selection of interesting sightings from the past seventy years, sightings that are well documented and were observed by a number of eyewitnesses. During my more than thirty-year career as a journalist, I have documented numerous UFO sightings, spoken to eyewitnesses, and am even able to present credibility of these witnesses; what struck me, is that in ninety-nine percent of all cases, the witnesses are credible and only told me what they actually saw with their own eyes. Additionally, we are in no way dealing with any publicity-hungry contemporaries who want to make a media splash with their stories. Often, the opposite was the case—the witnesses even asked me to omit their full names and any photos, since they did not want to expose themselves to ridicule.

In the following pages, I want to attempt to get on the track of the truth, or at least get closer to it. You will read about exciting cases and the stories of eyewitnesses who have observed strange things—things that belong to the great unsolved mysteries between heaven and Earth. If you also have once been a witness to an extraordinary sighting, write me and tell me your story. I look forward to your letters.

—Frank Schwede
Autumn 2014

Introduction

A Class A UFO: A flying saucer with a solid structure. Snapshot taken on a clear day. (Schwede archive)

You may notice right away: This is not a typical research book. It lacks the familiar data tables with all the important information on dimensions and speed, and in this case also, our usually profuse photographic material turns out to be rather thin. But the title "UFOs" should already give you some insight. UFOs are *unidentified flying objects* and, accordingly, we lack verified data or even outline drawings. And the photos also are a bit of a difficulty. Although there is a large number of images in this digital age, as a rule, we should appreciate them cautiously. Technology, as is well known, makes all kinds of manipulation and falsification possible, so in this volume, I was usually limited to material that has been at least halfway "verified" over the

years, even if it is of a quality often insufficient for present day requirements for illustrations.

But first let me clarify the concept of "unidentified." Unidentified is, to begin with, everything you can neither interpret nor explain or see clearly at first glance. This can be an aircraft flying at high altitude, which, by reflecting sunbeams, sends peculiar light beams to the ground; a helicopter flying at night with its searchlights on, which cannot be heard due to the wind direction; or brightly lit planets or stars, such as Venus, shining behind a thin layer of clouds and emitting a strange distorted light. Just from these examples, we can very easily recognize that UFOs are not necessarily extraterrestrial or just some little "green men" visiting our Earth.

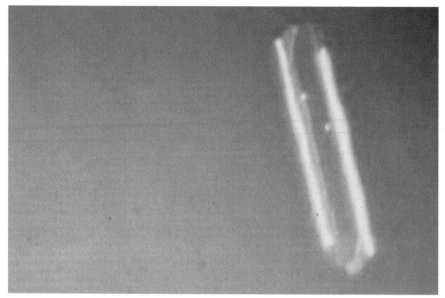

In this image it remains unclear whether this is a body with a solid structure, a solar balloon, or simply a cloud or part of a dissolving strip of condensation. The tubular object looks transparent and translucent—as pilots often describe unidentified flying objects. (Schwede archive)

However, during the past forty years, the term "UFO" has always been put in a corner, which hasn't done the issue any good up to the present. Thus, scholarly science has preferred to distance itself from this issue, so that only so-called esoteric scientists grapple with the subject and repeatedly see themselves as subject to hostility. There is hardly any topic with such a bad reputation, and journalists and authors who deal with UFOs have to fear for their reputations. The group of those who believe that unidentifiable flying objects are merely illusions or fantasies and exist only in eyewitnesses' minds and imaginations, is a large one. Thus, explanation should consist in investigating why people have seen what they describe. The group of esoteric scientists, by contrast, believes that the witnesses are only describing what they have actually seen and seek a logical and plausible explanation involving all options—thus, what kind of object the eyewitnesses actually saw (such as the above-mentioned evening star, a hot air balloon at a great height, or the landing lights of an approaching aircraft in the far distance, making no noticeable engine noise). It is particularly difficult to assess whether, at the time of the sighting, it is possible to rule out either meteorological influences such as lightning, northern lights, or some invasive weather conditions, and if the object was simultaneously visible as a radar signal. Some case studies will be explained in the following chapters. Scientists who deal with the evaluation of sightings must not only be able to accurately assess the sources of the observations come, but also be well versed in the psychology of perception, meteorology, astronomy, physics, and aerospace-missile technology.

In general, UFO sightings are divided into three classes:

Class A: Unidentifiable flying objects with solid structures.

Class B: Lights, spheres, or glowing masses.

Class C: Paranormal luminous phenomena that appear at special places, such as religious centers, and in the surroundings of people with paranormal abilities.

For scholarly science, these three classes do not exist, because they are misunderstood in the eyes of serious scientists, who, therefore, still today attach no importance to them. It is really in the nature of things, that when a flying object that is unknown to the viewer is sighted, the first step should be to go into all logical explanations. Furthermore, scholarly science should realize that scientific thinking also means considering what cannot be explained causally to begin with. Thus, scholarly science should consider theories that might sound a bit abstract or even absurd at first glance, but on the other side shouldn't be excluded, because the opposite is not or not yet proven. In most countries, serious UFO research is still in its infancy today, or is deliberately dismissed by the varied governments as unimportant. At this time, France is the only country in Europe that acknowledges to its citizens that it takes UFO phenomenon seriously, and they are the subject of government-funded investigation. In 1977, the French space agency Centre National d'Etudes Spatiales (CNES) [National Center of Space Studies] set up a special department that deals with the direct investigation of the UFO phenomenon. With this, CNES became the first government authority in the world that uses public funding to investigate the phenomenon. The goal of these investigations was, among other things, to indicate to the population that the phenomenon will be taken seriously. The first officially reported UFO sighting occurred in France in 1937. But only since the 1950s, has there been a real boost in observations of unexplained heavenly phenomena.

On its website, the CNES lists 6,000 people who reportedly made about 1,600 observations in France, for which they could find no conclusive explanation. However, the researchers soon found, after analyzing the existing images and film material, there were totally natural explanations.

Two children watching a flying saucer. The image likely comes from the mid-1950s or early 1960s. Unfortunately, it is not known where the picture was taken or whether it is a fake or photo montage. (Schwede archive)

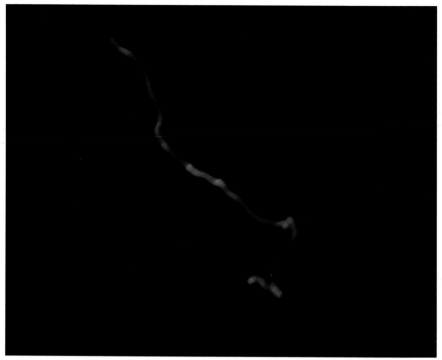

Picture of a red "fireball" taken by the author in 2012 over Feldafng on Lake Starnberg. The object hovered across the evening sky from west to east silently, three times at an interval of two minutes, at an altitude of around .3 miles (500 meters). Similar objects are spotted around the world time and again. (Schwede archive)

In only thirty-six percent of cases no explicable cause of the occurrence of the object shown could be found. And in thirteen and one-half percent there were no rational explanations. This fact brought the former head of the CNES Group, Jean-Jacques Velasco, to state: "Yes, UFOs exist. And they are of extraterrestrial origin."

Once we accept this once without a value judgment, then comes recurring question: Where do the visitors come from? There are three classic hypotheses.

1. Extraterrestrial

The UFOs are spaceships, which have been developed and built by an alien and industrially highly developed civilization and travel from their home planet through space to earth. They may possibly come from a large mothership that is "moored" somewhere in space. But in today's perspective, there are good reasons against this thesis. Space travel faster than the speed of light is impossible at our present state of knowledge.

2. Visitors from the Future

The visitors and their flying machines come from the future and manage to travel through time. That would also be a possible explanation for why UFOs have been sighted in all eras. (More on this in the chapter "And They Came in Fiery Chariots.")

The Avro Canada VZ-9AV "Avrocar" was initially a Canadian military project; from 1953, it was in the hands of the US Air Force under the code name "Project Silver Bug." The Avro resembled a flying saucer and had vertical take-off and landing capabilities. However, the disk was unstable over about four feet (0.9 meters) in the air, and engine performance was weak. Above the ground, the disk could reach a maximum speed of about thirty mph (forty-eight km/h). In December 1961, the project was finally abandoned. (US Air Force)

3. Visitors from Parallel Universes

Due to, for us so far, completely unknown physics, the visitors are able to penetrate the dimensional barrier between ours, and anothers, to get to our universe or in our vicinity. This hypothesis is advocated by French physicist Jacques Vallée, but here, too, so far the necessary evidence that there are any parallel universes existing is lacking.

But why is there no effort on the part of scholarly science to investigate the UFO phenomenon in the face of these questions?

For many, the answer may be obvious: How do you investigate something for which there is no tangible and, above all, no material evidence? This is why most scientists would rather leave it alone. A reputation still counts a lot in the scientific community today. In addition, there is no global network of monitoring stations with cameras, magnetometers, and radar antennas. These would be necessary to detect the phenomena that appear at various points of the earth at unpredictable times and then vanish again. Facilities of such a magnitude are expensive, and national governments not only obviously

9

UFO or natural phenomenon? Nighttime UFO sighting. At night, it is often difficult to make a serious judgment about a light phenomenon. Auroras, noctilucent clouds, planes, or comets are often possible natural explanations. (Schwede archive)

lack the necessary financial resources, but also the motivation to create a network of this kind. Renowned physics professor August Meessen of the Catholic University of Leuven (Belgium) cannot understand this attitude on the part of many countries in terms of UFO research. In his work, "The study of physical aspects of the UFO phenomenon," Meessen advocates the view that

On November 17, 1974, H. Lauersen photographed this "jellyfish-like" disk in Viborg, Denmark. The case was officially investigated by the Danish Air Force. Since the surface of the object was apparently extremely cold, the immediate ambient atmosphere vaporized and flowed to the ground, which gave the disk this strange appearance. (H. Lauersen)

science could definitely develop further by investigating the UFO phenomenon. Meessen believes, namely, that the UFO phenomenon is not irrational, but instead physically real and thus accessible to research. This opinion is also advocated by US astrophysicist Bernard Haisch: "New physical findings suggest that interstellar travel does not appear to be as impossible as previously thought."

Haisch also considers it conceivable that extraterrestrials have long been on Earth and have not revealed themselves as such for a

number of reasons. Therefore, it would be only logical and consistent, according to Haisch, to search for evidence of the visitors. Haisch: "Only this way can we tell if we aren't already part of the Galactic Club without knowing it."

But a "visiting alien" does not have to necessarily be behind every sighted flying object. In many cases, we are dealing simply with secret test aircraft, which the governments of the respective countries want to remain silent about, for understandable reasons. Reports from Belgium in 1989, for example, could in truth be traced back to a top-secret air-superiority aircraft of the US Aurora program, developed already at the beginning of the 1980s, which was supposedly tested at the time and also flew to European NATO bases. After all, triangles were increasingly observed during the following years all over the world, even in the former Soviet Union. (More on this in the chapter entitled "The Secret of the Black Triangles.") This book will attempt to show all possibilities that can be concealed behind the sighting of unidentified flying objects. That observations and descriptions of an object by several persons on the ground can turn out to be quite different, may explain the following example: A hiking group is on a night excursion. It's a starry night and, during a short break, one of the participants in the group observes a strange light in the southwestern sky. The alleged object in the sky quickly becomes a fixed point for the observer and his gaze remains on the luminous phenomenon for more than five minutes. All of a sudden, the observer sees that the strange light is moving, dancing back and forth, and performing odd flying movements. After a while, he makes the others in the group aware of the strange dancing light. Eagerly, they now all direct their attention to the red dot in the evening sky. Meanwhile, a thin cirrostratus cloud has moved in front of the light phenomenon, so that the light-point appears distorted to the observers. Suddenly, the round light has become a sort of milky, yellowish glowing ellipse and the witnesses now speak of an object that has changed in color and shape. After extensive research, however, it soon turns out that the eyewitnesses have merely observed the evening star. Due to the cirrostratus cloud, the color and shape changed slightly and the dancing movements seen by one witness can be explained because of a slight tremor of the eye muscles from prolonged staring at a distant object.

Of course, not all sightings can be explained so simply and quickly. There are definitely also apparitions and objects in the daytime as well as in the night sky, which often can never be fully explained, as one case in the next chapter, which now dates back more than thirty years.

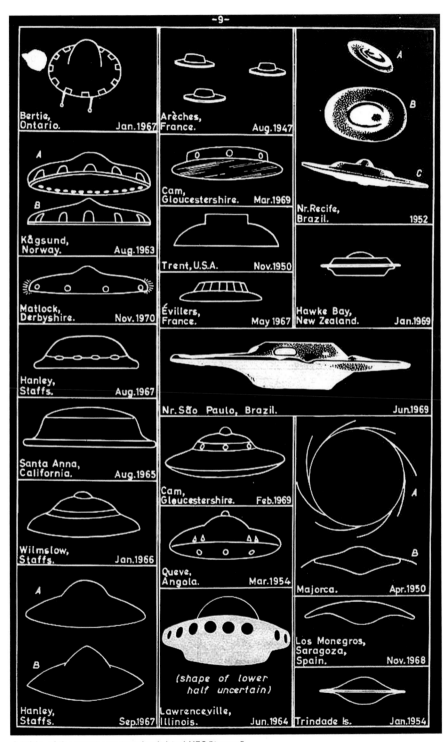

-9-

Bertie, Ontario. Jan.1967	Arèches, France. Aug.1947	Nr.Recife, Brazil. 1952
Kågsund, Norway. Aug.1963	Cam, Gloucestershire. Mar.1969	
Matlock, Derbyshire. Nov.1970	Trent, U.S.A. Nov.1950	Hawke Bay, New Zealand. Jan.1969
Hanley, Staffs. Aug.1967	Évillers, France. May 1967	
Santa Anna, California. Aug.1965	Nr. São Paulo, Brazil. Jun.1969	Majorca. Apr.1950
Wilmslow, Staffs. Jan.1966	Cam, Gloucestershire. Feb.1969	Los Monegros, Saragoza, Spain. Nov.1968
Hanley, Staffs. Sep.1967	Queve, Angola. Mar.1954	
	(shape of lower half uncertain) Lawrenceville, Illinois. Jun.1964	Trindade Is. Jan.1954

A table of the most commonly sighted UFO "types."

1. UFOs Over Germany

March 12, 1982, a Friday: Students Manuela H. (14) and Sonja B. (15) from Messel near Darmstadt, were on their way home from a party. The two girls had to be home not later than ten, as they had agreed with their parents, and they kept to it. It was shortly after nine o'clock p.m., when the students left a classmate's birthday party. The two girls joked around on the approximate fifteen-minute walk.

Suddenly, Sonja cried out: "Hey, look at the light up there, what's that?"

Now Manuela also saw the strange light and became frightened. The glaring light kept coming down closer—until it was finally at treetop height, then pulled back up again, to fall down back toward the two girls in the next moment.

Manuela found the thing scary, and then cried out to her friend: "Let's get out of here, I'm scared."

Panic-stricken, the two teenagers fled to a nearby school, where a dance for local young people was just going on, with Manuela's brother Werner (seventeen) among them. Distraught, the girls reported what they had just witnessed and were picked up by their parents.

About a quarter of an hour later, more young people left the dance—including Manuela's brother, Werner. Their attention, too, was immediately attracted by the bright light in the direction of a nearby playground. Curious, the group ran up to the light and saw, floating in the sky about 1,968 feet (600 meters) above the trees, a glowing blue plate with a diameter of approximately thirty-two feet (ten meters) and an oblong or oval underside. Atop it, the students dimly recognized a dome, which was bathed in a dazzling light, and in it, something was turning—like a beacon. One after the other, the colors shone yellow, green, and red. At the edge of the plate were four square lights, at equal distances from each other. On the underside of the disk, a quite thick protrusion could be seen, which off and on emitted a bluish-white cone of light. The teenagers were approximately 130 feet (forty meters) distant from the spectacle going on in front of them and were so fascinated that it took a full ten minutes before they came back to their senses, due to a bright, bluish flash, followed by a thud. In the same hour, in the living rooms of Messel, Neu Kranichstein and the adjacent suburbs of Darmstadt, the television set images became blurry. Inexplicable radar signals appeared on the radar screens of the military air traffic control of US strike forces in Frankfurt. Four unidentified flying objects were seen on the radar screens making their way over Messel to Darmstadt. Approximately half-an-hour later, they had disappeared without trace. At least, this is how it was reported a few days later in the *Darmstadt Tagblatt.*

Around 9:30 p.m., the uncanny object was also spotted by a Darmstadt police radio car team, as a green-white dot hovering above the trees. "It was as big as two stars, but much brighter, and it kept changing color from dark green to bright green to almost white; behind it were four other bodies," Police Chief Thomas Weiland later told reporters at the Arheilgen police station. Someone who also claims to have seen the object is local community nurse Margaret Gustafson from Messel. On March 16, 1982, she reported her sighting on the ZDF (Zweites Deutsches Ferhsehn: Second German TV channel) program *Drehscheibe* [*Hub*] in the following words:

> At first, my husband and I only saw a terribly bright flash and heard a rumble, and I thought, of course, of weather lightning. I tried to calm my boy, because he was totally beside himself, and then I said, there are no UFOs; they don't exist, and we went to the other boys to reassure them—they were all pretty freaked out. At first I thought they were probably drunk or something, because they had been at the disco, and then we are back at home, after everyone had scattered, and then we saw, alongside our flat bungalow, a light over the building, as big as, of the dimensions of a star, that's how I would rate it; sort of orange-deep red, and it disappeared with lightning speed, and came back towards us thirty-two feet (ten meters) lower; it kept getting bigger, disappeared again, moved upwards, and came towards us again. And since my husband and I couldn't explain this, we were really frightened. And then I called the police.

The whole thing has remained a mystery until today. Only a group of amateur researchers from Mannheim believed, a short time later, that they had found an explanation for the strange light phenomena in the sky over Darmstadt. They surmised that the explanation for the Messel UFO were the three planets Jupiter, Mars, and Saturn, which were almost lined up in the sky

at the beginning of 1982; the rest was just coincidence and associated with a good dose of fantasy.

This case is undoubtedly among the well-documented UFO reports from Germany; however, as so often is the case with descriptions of UFOs, it leaves a lot of questions unanswered. What had the young people, the eight officers, and the community nurse really seen that night? Certainly no planetary alignment. The objects were simply too close to the observers for that, and besides, planets don't leave any traces on air traffic control radar screens and, in particular, don't cause any TV interference. In the end, the explanations are also sketchy, as always. It was attempted to cite all possible natural explanations: from a hot air balloon, to flying Chinese lanterns, all the way to remote-controlled model airplanes.

In the following report also, many eyewitnesses ultimately questioned whether what they saw actually happened, or finally was just their imaginations. But in this case, there were dozens of eyewitnesses who all saw the same thing: spheres that cavorted across the evening sky over Greifswald on the evening of August 24, 1990, executing strange movements. No one knew, at the time in question, that the dancing balls of light would trigger such a media response. At first, Valeri Vinogradov also thought nothing about it, when he briefly looked out the window during his evening meal and saw the objects over the Baltic Sea. It was only when his wife said, about a quarter-of-an-hour later, that people outside in the courtyard were talking about UFOs, that he looked more closely at the sky again. In fact, there *was* something there: first four, then six, and finally seven orange-red balls. One after another, they flared up and suddenly disappeared

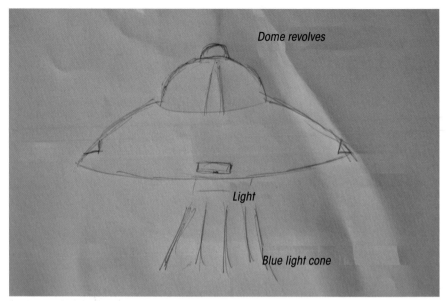

Freehand sketch of Messel UFO. In the dome, there was reportedly some kind of beacon turning, showing the colors yellow, green and red; there were angular lights on the edges. A bluish-white cone of light came from a protrusion on the underside.

again—as if someone had turned off the light switch.

More than a hundred people witnessed this show over Greifswald live for hours—including nuclear physicists from the nuclear power plant in Greifswald, tourists, and locals. Many of them used video cameras to film the strange-looking maneuvers of the balls of light from different perspectives. The couple Ludmilla and Nikolai Ivanov even recorded the objects from their second-floor apartment on video and were finally completely fascinated by the spectacle it provided them.

But the unknown flying objects over Rostock didn't just provoke fascination among the observers. Many people panicked. Among them, fifteen holiday guests of the "Solidarity" guest house. The vacationers later reported to journalists that they had been upset by strange lights that remained for several minutes over the water and disappeared again as suddenly as they had come. Some of them ultimately believed they had hallucinated; others spoke of a whole invasion of "aliens." Computer specialists from the group MUFONCES (Mutual UFO Network—Central European Section) finally succeeded in determining by triangulation (angle determination) the exact location and especially the size of the objects. The analysis revealed that the group of lights had remained stationary over a small island about three to four miles (5–8 km) north of Peenemunde. This was the position of a former military base, where Wernher von Braun, among others, had carried out tests with his V2 rockets

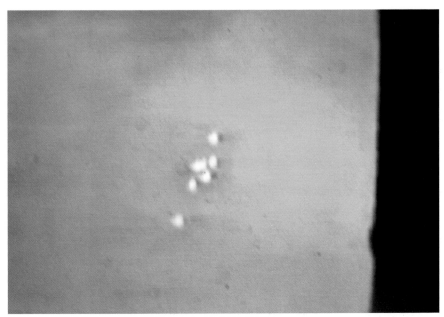

MUFON CES calculated that the group of lights was about 3 miles (approximately 5,000 meters) in the air, around 15 miles (24 km) northeast of Greifswald. The second group was around 16,400 feet (5,600 meters) in the air and located about 15.5 miles (25 km) from Greifswald. The size of the spheres is estimated to be about 6.5 feet – 40 feet (2–12 meters) in diameter.

in World War II. After the war, there was a Soviet base there.

According to the calculation, the group of lights meandered at about three miles (5,000 meters) in the air, around fifteen miles (twenty-four km) northeast of Greifswald. The second group remained at around three and one-half miles (5,600 meters) in the air and about fifteen and one-half miles (twenty-five km) northeast from Greifswald. Based on this data, it was possible to estimate the size of the spheres at about 6.5 feet – 40 feet (2–12 meters) in diameter.

The next day, *Bild* newspaper reported that there had probably been an "extraterrestrial inspection above the notorious nuclear power plant at Greifswald." But ultimately, the lights of Greifswald were more than just a "joke article" in Germany's biggest tabloid. More than that, they remained a mystery even for scientists for a long time. Various causes were considered, including light reflections, but soon, due to the fact that different observers indeed did see the phenomenon from different directions, these were ruled out. Other eyewitnesses, especially locals, wanted to identify the strange lights as

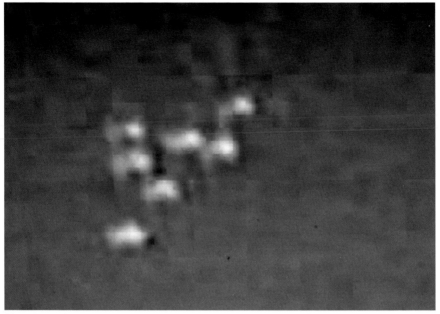

More than a hundred people witnessed the strange spectacle live for hours—some eyewitnesses filmed the whole thing with their video cameras from different perspectives.

just practice ammunition of the former NVA [National Volksaremme: the East German armed forces]—as stated by skipper Erwin K., who sailed his ferry between the mainland and Rügen that evening. When he looked over in the direction of the Bay of Greifswald, he also saw that strange group of lights high in the sky, but at second glance, they reminded him more of earlier times, when the armed forces of the former Volksarmee [People's Army] often held day-long maneuvers in this region, shooting flares into the evening sky. Another person who has also worked extensively on the Greifswald lights is Munich astrophysicist Illobrand von Ludwiger of the MUFONCES group. For him, at any rate, flares can be eliminated, due to their properties as follows: The duration of their appearance—two of the objects of the second group were visible for at least ten minutes—the emergence of new balls of light in the second group, the first group's vanishing together, and the spontaneous and synchronous movement of all the objects in a group. Von Ludwiger was also able to report that such balls of light have been observed at many places on Earth. This is particularly common in Russia, in an area around Tbilisi and near Perm. Near the Ural Mountains, east of Perm, lies the Molyobka or M-triangle, where numerous expeditions have already been made to investigate light phenomena of this kind—but so far, without tangible results.

So, will the lights over Greifswald forever remain a mystery?

No, claims Dennis Kirstein and Jochen Ickinger of the group "UfoInformation." They hold that the mystery of Greifswald has been solved for a long time. In their final report on the spectacle over the Baltic Sea, the two researchers come to the unanimous conclusion that on that said evening of August 24, there was an exercise of the Czech Armed Forces, during which, among other things, type SAB flare bombs (lighting material suspended from a parachute to illuminate target or combat areas) were used, which were shot in the air as an exercise target. Dr. Ludger S. was mentioned as a witness in this report; he was sailing that evening in his dinghy by the Eiland Greifswalder Oie [Greifswald Isle]. He assumed that the flares were initially shot into the air from the seaward side, using small rockets aboard a warship, and then individually flared up in a rough formation and floated slowly on oversized parachutes into the ascending thermal updraft from the warmed Baltic. However, S. had not seen the process himself, but, according to his information, knew of this phenomenon from his time in the NVA. He told UfoInformation:

This phenomenon is known to nighttime sailors in our area. To me, there were no UFOs, never ever. In addition, I've seen them too often out there. Also, as a former NVA officer, I participated in them several times myself, when you shot up these targets, called "pine trees" in our insider jargon. You must know that these flares go very high, and then serve as practice targets for infrared sensing ground-to-air missiles; you can't exactly practice on real aircraft. In the current case, the missiles used were clearly coming from Polish territory. On one film you can even see the explosions—in the form of short flashes of light—of such missiles. You will now ask me why the rocket fire tail of the oncoming projectiles is not to be seen. This is very easy to explain. During

the firing on the ground and during about half their flight time, these fire tails are clearly visible, then the rocket flies a good distance further, borne solely by thrust and just the after-flow of their exhaust plume. Then the light targets were extinguished, in approximately the reverse order to their appearance. I had already seen this on TV, but thought that officials would have already clarified the matter; that's why I did not report it. Only your call made me realize that this is still regarded as a UFO. In my opinion, it is nonsensical to mystify this phenomenon.

For Illobrand von Ludwiger from MUFONCES, the riddle of the Greifswald lights is by no means clarified. He has also included the possibility that flares were being used in his deliberations and investigations. But for MUFONCES, this option is definitely ruled out. Von Ludwiger verbatim:

The MUFONCES investigators also had thorough knowledge about the phenomena of flare cartridges from research near the Grafenwöhr military training area of Grafenwöhr. The Greifswald lights are different from flare cartridges, not only in their size and absolutely round shape, but also in an effect, which the critics are concealing, and caused headaches for the scientists of MUFONCES and those from the Max Planck Institute for Aeronomy in Lindau (Harz): in the second group of eight spheres, small objects repeatedly approached, remained in place there, flew out again and some came back again. This could not be a matter of flare cartridges, since these would not slow down, but fly through

Many UFO researchers hold that it was conceivable that flares were being used. However, according to a statement from Illobrand von Ludwiger, the light balls' ability to maneuver definitely excludes this explanation. The picture shows the deployment of flares, as they are used by armed forces around the world. (US Navy)

the group of lights. Incidentally, no German, Pole, Russian, or Czech has ever since been found, who would share being present at any supposed shooting of flares at that time. MUFONCES had offered an approximate $3,100 (3,000 DEM) reward for anyone who could produce a witness."

The search for the truth in the case of the Greifswald lights continues.

It is questionable whether the puzzle can ever be completely solved twenty-five years later. It is often the bewildering variety of reported objects that baffles research. Sometimes it is luminous phenomena in the form of spheres or balls of light that appear alone or in whole groups and maneuver in the sky, disappear, and reappear, as described in the case of Greifswald; then there are objects described as disks or cigar-shaped, some chasing through the air at an unbelievable speed. Other witnesses even describe encounters with UFOs that have landed and had contact with their crew.

Not too long ago, there was an increasing number of media reports that contained stories of abductions by UFO crews; there were even many such cases from Germany. Alleged victims reported all kinds of experiments; some of those abducted spoke of having been contaminated and being left permanently damaged. Many of the witnesses could only remember the experience under hypnosis, while others in turn reported supernatural capabilities they have acquired after their encounters with UFOs.

Skeptics often like to ask the following question here: Are UFOs a modern phenomenon, or did some people already have encounters with objects of this kind in antiquity or even earlier? This can be answered with a clear yes. In reality, the UFO phenomenon is perhaps as old as human history, as the reports in the next chapter show.

2. And They Came in Fiery Chariots

Ever since mankind has been trying to understand the things that he sees in the heavens, he again and again has encountered phenomena that he cannot easily explain right away. In the late Middle Ages and antiquity, scribes championed the view that astronomical objects are signs, and are not real existing bodies and objects. This first changed with the Age of Enlightenment; only then did men recognize the true cause for the appearance of celestial bodies in the forms of meteorites, fireballs, and other things—even the aurora long remained a mystery shrouded in secrecy—the riddle was only solved through the discovery of the corpuscular radiation coming from the sun in the fourth decade of the last century. We embark on a journey back to the Old Stone Age: 30,000 BC to 10,000 BC. During this period, a people whose direct descendants are the present-day Basques, created artistic masterpieces of painting and sculpture, which can be seen today in seventeen prehistoric caves in southern France and northern Spain. They show exact depictions of humans and animals, but also include strange representations and things for which there are no logical explanation, at least at first glance. These works include more than forty different types of strange objects whose shapes resemble in an astonishing way those objects that we commonly would refer to as UFOs today—among them "machines" with long

Did the Prophet Ezekiel really see a spaceship in 586 BC while in Babylonian captivity? ". . . A stormy wind came out of the north, and a great cloud, with brightness around it, and fire flashing forth continually, and in the midst of the fire, as it were gleaming silver metal. And from the midst of it came the likeness of four living creatures. They had a human likeness." (Eze. 1, 1–5)

landing legs and circular hatches. Many archaeologists and speleologists today are certain the artists from that era only recreated in true to nature form—what they really saw—and these cave paintings are thus assessed as trustworthy. But for skeptics, this fact is not quite so sure. For them, it is clear that modern man can interpret everything in the cave paintings based on his present state of knowledge, and when ultimately it's just a matter of his subjective imagination, then perhaps a harmless egg can suddenly become a UFO.

Similar motifs can also be found, incidentally, outside the Pyrenees area. It quickly also becomes obvious when studying the Bible that everything is just a matter of interpretation and your own imagination. Here again, there are numerous passages that easily allow us to think of the descriptions in modern UFO reports—for example, the prophet Ezekiel, who was in Babylonian captivity, when he had the following experience in 586 BC:

> On the fifth day of the fourth month in my thirtieth year, while I was among the exiles by the Kebar River, a stormy wind came out of the north, and a great cloud, with brightness around it, and fire flashing forth continually, and in the midst of the fire, as it were gleaming silver metal. And from the midst of it came the likeness of four living creatures. They had human form. (Eze. 1, 1-5)

Did Ezekiel really see a flying spaceship, from which astronauts emerged in human form? There are possible indications of extraterrestrial visitors in other places in the Bible. For example, on their flight from Egypt, the people of Israel were led by a pillar of cloud that became a pillar of fire at night. And the prophet Elijah was possibly fetched away by a fiery chariot of fire and rode up to heaven in a whirlwind. Even Pharaoh Thutmose the Third in 1450 BC saw circles of fire in the sky. The Roman writer Julius Obsequens

also reported about "things like ships" and a "golden globe of fire" in the sky.

In Japan, as well, there was a first documented sighting in the year 1235. On the night of September 24, strange lights suddenly appeared in the sky, which swung back and forth in circular form and could be observed long into the early morning hours. Shogun Kujo Yoritsune even ordered a scientific study of the occurrence—but with the sobering result that it was probably just the wind that must have moved the stars back and forth.

In the year 322 BC, Alexander the Great besieged the Phoenician fortress of Tyre—the approximately fifty-five-foot-high (seventeen meters) walls were considered impregnable. But what happened with Alexander's army during the seventh month of the siege truly sounds amazing:

> One day suddenly these flying shields, as they were called, appeared over the camp of the Macedonians. They flew in triangular formations, led at the front by a very large one; the others were only half as large. Altogether there were five. Slowly they circled over Tyre, while thousands of warriors on both sides broke off the fight and watched in amazement. Suddenly a flash of light came from the largest ship, which struck into the walls and made them collapse; other flashes followed and destroyed walls and towers, as if they were made of clay, and opened the way for the attackers (...). The flying shields circled again above the city (...) then they disappeared quickly upwards, until they soon disappeared in the blue sky.

Just what the observers saw over Tyre is still a mystery—but the tradition reads almost as if the army of Alexander the Great was supported by modern technology that used rays to collapse the walls and towers. UFO reports, therefore,

An illustration from the "Nürnberger Flugblatt" [Nuremberg broadsheet]. On April 14, 1561, hundreds of people saw strange spheres in the night sky over the Franconian city of Nuremberg. The objects were shaped like spheres, crosses, disks and tubes. (Zurich Central Library)

aren't just modern ravings, attributable to some science fiction stories. The people of earlier eras also saw such things, and they captured and described these in words. But their power of imagination was just not sufficient to represent these as visitors from a distant galaxy—for the people of the ancient world, these objects usually had a divine origin. The most prominent UFO sighting in early modern times took place at night on April 14, 1561, in the Franconian city of Nuremberg. Hundreds of Nurembergers saw strange spheres in the night sky over this fortress town. The objects were not just spherical in shape, but shapes like crosses, disks, and tubes also appeared to the fascinated and distraught people, and they began, according to eyewitness accounts, "to contend with each other." The heavenly spectacle lasted for about an hour—subsequently, the objects "fell from heaven to

the Earth, as if they were burning," and "gradually vanished with a lot of steam." One of the eyewitnesses was book printer Hanns Glaser, who describes his observations in his so-called "Nürnberger Flugblatt" (Nuremberg leaflet) in the following words:

> There were spheres of blood-red, bluish, and iron black color or ring disks in large numbers, roughly in a line, sometimes four in a square, also some by themselves, and between such spheres also some blood-colored crosses were to be seen.

Five years later, in 1566, Samuel Coccius reported a similar observation in a broadsheet (similar to a newspaper but printed only on one side) from Basel. There, on the morning of August 7, a large number of black spheres were

In 1566, Samuel Coccius reported in a Basel broadsheet about a sighting on the morning of August 7. Many Basel inhabitants saw black spheres in the sky, which were "performing rapid movements and running into each other, as if they were having a fight."

reportedly seen in the sky by many inhabitants of Basel; these were performing rapid movements, flying in curves, and at times running into each other "as if they were having a fight." According to a report that has been handed down, after a certain time, the spheres began to glow red and then were extinguished. The "sun miracle of Fatima," in the early twentieth century, can also be interpreted as a UFO sighting. Because of a prophecy, on October 13, 1917, more than 30,000 people gathered in Portugal's Cova da Iria near Fatima, to witness the last visit of the Virgin Mary. According to eyewitnesses, after a heavy rain shower the clouds reportedly broke and the sun appeared as a transparent, rotating disk for around ten minutes. The natural scientist Professor Dr. Garret Almeida of the University of Coimbra describes the event in the following words:

The sun disk did not remain still. This was not the twinkling of a heavenly body, because it whirled around itself in a wild vortex, when suddenly a noise was heard by everyone. The sun seemed, whirling, to dissolve from the firmament and to threateningly draw nearer to the ground, as if to crush us with its huge fiery weight. The sensation during those moments was terrible.

Even recognized authorities of the respective periods have reported again and again about strange and unexplained objects in the sky. Thus, on October 10, 1864, famous French astronomer Leverier saw a shining tube-shaped object in the sky over Paris. Its origin has also never been explained. On June 12, 1790, a huge fire-red

Fresco in a monastery church in Kosovo. Fantasy or reality? Have foreign visitors already been on Earth in all epochs?

globe plummeted from the heavens near the French city of Alencon. It grazed a hill and, soon after the crash, set everything around it on fire. Many residents rushed out to the crash site, where they found a strange object with a door from which a man emerged and fled. Soon afterward, the object literally dissolved into thin air, leaving behind only a pile of ashes. The case was later thoroughly investigated by a police prefecture in Paris, but Inspector Liabeuf, commissioned with the investigation, was never able to solve the case.

3. Searching for Traces

Deep in the Cheyenne Mountains in the US state of Colorado is NORAD (North American Aerospace Defense Command), the central command post for air defense and early warning of the American and Canadian Air Forces. NORAD's "eyes and ears" are extensive—in addition to aerial surveillance, they also turn their gaze towards outer space. Here they watch for missiles, space junk, or possible groups of attackers on their way to the US or Canada. At times, however, NORAD operators see something more on their radar screens, namely objects for which, at first glance, there is no explanation—objects whose flight characteristics correspond neither to those of satellites nor missiles or conventional aircraft. The NORAD sensors detect on average more than 500 of these objects annually. Whatever

they are, explaining them is laborious and time-consuming, and sometimes they remain enigmatic. To begin with, the sighted objects are often just radar signals that can mean anything and do not necessarily have to involve an optical sighting—signals that almost every air traffic control staff person around the world has already encountered on his radar screen at some point in his career and which often mean nothing, disappearing after a short time and may never re-emerge. But for reasons of flight safety, these traces must be followed up, when signals occur, for example, in the area of an airport's approach path. In the worst case, the result is immediate closure of the airspace, as in the following case.

On the evening of January 6, 2014, at around 6:00 p.m., suddenly a mysterious radar signal

Deep in the Cheyenne Mountains in Colorado is NORAD (North American Aerospace Defense Command), the central command post for air defense and early warning of the American and Canadian Air Forces. (US Government)

A look into the NORAD command center. Here is where it all comes together. (US Government)

NORAD operators have repeatedly seen objects on their radar screens for which they could find no explanation—objects whose flight characteristics correspond neither to those of satellites nor missiles or conventional aircraft. (US Government)

appeared on the radar of the Bremen airport air traffic control. None of the air traffic control staff found an explanation for what was moving on the radar screen. The tower crew immediately directed their binoculars to the pitch-dark evening sky, where they actually saw a mysterious light maneuvering directly over the airport facilities.

No one knew, at the time in question, what consequences this phenomenon over Bremen might have for passengers on arriving aircraft this evening. One of the affected passengers described his impressions: At about 7:00 p.m., the self-employed businessman boarded the Boeing 737 for Lufthansa flight LH 2116 at

On the evening of January 6, 2014, a mysterious radar signal appeared on the Bremen Airport air traffic control radar at about 6:00 p.m.; none of the air traffic control employees found any explanation. Picture of the Bremen Airport tower. (Garitzko)

The main building of the Bremen Airport. (Tarawneh)

Looking into the sky is part of the daily routine for air traffic controllers. (Axel Péju)

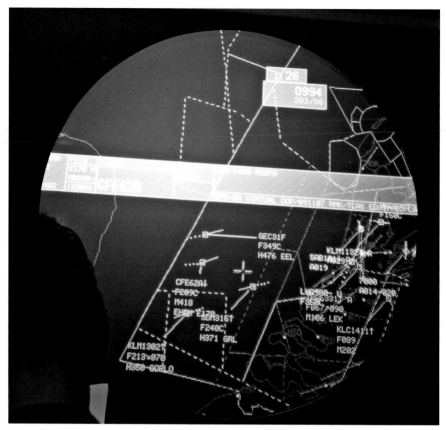

Air traffic controllers, of course, watch the radar as well. Unidentified radar signals are not uncommon, but in most cases they turn out to be harmless. (Wikimedia)

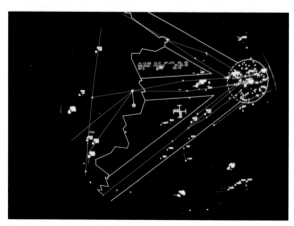

Radar image of the Berlin air corridors in 1989. (Wikimedia)

A Boeing 737-300, which was also in service in Flight LH 2116. Due to an unknown flying object near the airport flight holding patterns over Bremen, the jet, with seventy-six passengers on board, had to turn and was eventually diverted to Hanover. (Brian)

Munich Airport. The man from Bremen frequently had business in the Bavarian capital, and for him, flying was the fastest and most convenient means of transport. The flight time between Munich and Bremen is just over an hour. As the Boeing engines started, the passenger had long since retreated behind his daily newspaper. When he next looked at his watch, it was shortly before 9:00 p.m.; meanwhile, the Boeing has left its cruising altitude and was heading for Bremen Airport. In his mind, the forty-eight year old is already with his wife and daughter who are waiting for him at the airport, to pick him up by car, as always. But that night, everything would turn out differently: "We were in the direct landing approach when the pilot suddenly pulled the aircraft up again. At the time, we were told that a helicopter had crossed the flight path." The Lufthansa jet, with seventy-six passengers on board, turned in a holding pattern over Bremen and again entered the landing approach. But the second attempt also failed. The pilot now announced over the plane loudspeaker that the aircraft was on a direct collision course.

A flight attendant later explained things to the businessman and told him how risky the situation really was: "We were just fifteen seconds away from a collision with the UFO."

To this day, the witness still breaks into a sweat at the thought. He's a frequent flyer, flying somewhere in Germany or Europe almost every day, but he has never experienced anything like this. After two unsuccessful landing attempts, the aircraft flew in circles in the air above the vicinity of Bremen, until the pilot eventually flew to Hanover Airport.

Later, some passengers will testify that they could see a brightly shining, gyroscope-shaped object, which was completely motionless in the air; after some time it changed color and flew away, slowly at first and then faster. The UFO alert around the Bremen Airport on the evening of January 6, 2014, will certainly go down as one of the biggest UFO incidents in German history; never before had such an incident disrupted air traffic over an airport for a period of almost four hours.

The incident at Bremen didn't just create a great sensation in Germany; it also aroused the interest of many international media outlets.

Journalists from around the world called for Bremen police and asked for interviews, but to this day, the bewildered officials are unable to provide satisfactory answers about the uninvited visitors. Speculation surrounding the mysterious lights over the Bremen Airport dragged on for several weeks. The Bremen public prosecutor's office, together with the criminal police, analyzed reports from more than fifty witnesses and finally came to the following conclusion:

The still-unknown operator of the unidentified flying object is likely to be someone from the model airplane or multi-copter crowd. This is indicated by testimony from observers and experts. Some citizens may have observed and described the police helicopter used. Whistle-blowers from western Bremen will have seen an Air France aircraft in a holding pattern during the period when they were watching. This was a result of the Geo Data analysis ...

In a joint press release, the police and public prosecutors assume that a remote-controlled multi-copter was a possible cause of the strange lights over the Bremen Airport.

So much for the abbreviated police and public prosecutor's joint statement, which, however, left many questions open. According to the weather report, the wind in the Bremen area on the evening of January 6 was gusting up to force 4, which corresponds to an average rate of around twenty-five mph (forty km/h). That would mean that the alleged multi-copter must have gotten into serious turbulence due to its weight, which in turn would cause it to make jerky movements. In addition, the range of the radio transmitter used plays a critical role. Depending on the transmission power, the radio control of a model airplane moves in a radius of about 130 feet to 1.25 miles (300 to 2,000 meters). A further unresolved issue, according to a statement of the tower staff, is the alleged radar contact made, which in any case is unlikely to originate from a multi-copter. For an object to leave a radar echo on the radar screen requires a minimum size of a few square feet/meters, for it to be visible at all as a radar image. That means that, whatever the air traffic controllers sighted on their radar . . . it was certainly no multi-copter. Thus, open questions remain to this day.

The ghost light of the Bremen Airport is by no means an isolated case. Many times in the past, all but collisions have occurred between unidentified flying objects and airliners. One of the more recent examples is the dramatic sighting by the pilot of an Airbus A320 in the evening hours of July 19, 2013, approximately twelve and one-half miles (twenty kilometers) away from London Heathrow Airport. While the co-pilot was busy with the landing check, the first flight officer saw an object through the left window coming from the west, flying towards the Airbus at the same altitude. The pilot was immediately prepared for the worst and ducked reflexively

Kenneth Arnold stated that he saw a formation of bright objects over Mount Rainier that moved with almost unbelievable speed.

Mighty Mount Rainier in Washington State. Here, recreational pilot Kenneth Arnold saw a formation of unidentified flying objects on June 24, 1947. (Siegmund)

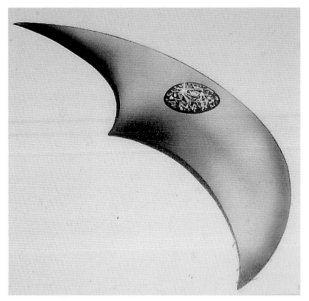

An artist's representation of the Arnold UFO.

toward the co-pilot's side, who had, however, witnessed nothing of the entire incident. According to the aircraft captain, it appeared like a cigar or rugby ball-shaped, metallic object. The description coincides roughly with that of an object that the former chief pilot of Lufthansa, Werner Utter, said he observed during a flight from New York to Frankfurt at approximately six and one-quarter miles (10,000 meters) above the Atlantic—and here, there was almost a collision. (More about the incident in the chapter entitled "UFO Sightings by Pilots.") UFO sightings of this kind are not modern figments of imagination, as we have already experienced in the previous chapter. But the issue of UFOs first really became popular since the late 1940s. In that decade, the term "flying saucer" first emerged in the United States—more precisely in Washington State on June 24, 1947: The thirty-two-year-old businessman Kenneth Arnold had come a long way as a fire extinguishing systems representative at Great Western Fire Control Supply. The company's

large number of customers appreciated Arnold's friendly, open, and uncomplicated manner and appreciated getting his advice. The customers ranged from a series of air charter companies to smaller sports airfields, often miles distant from each other. To visit his customers, Arnold almost always used his own sports aircraft—because flying was one of his great passions. In his younger years, the passionate amateur pilot had already racked up a lot of flight hours.

The hot June sun was already burning from a steel-blue sky since the early morning on that June 24; there was not a cloud in sight—ideal flying weather. Among Arnold's customers on this Tuesday was an airline near Chehalis in Washington State. Already in the late midday hours, earlier than planned, installation of the new fire extinguisher had been completed in the aircraft. Satisfied, Arnold looked at his watch and decided, since he still had plenty of time until his next appointment, that during his the return flight to Yakima, he would take part in the

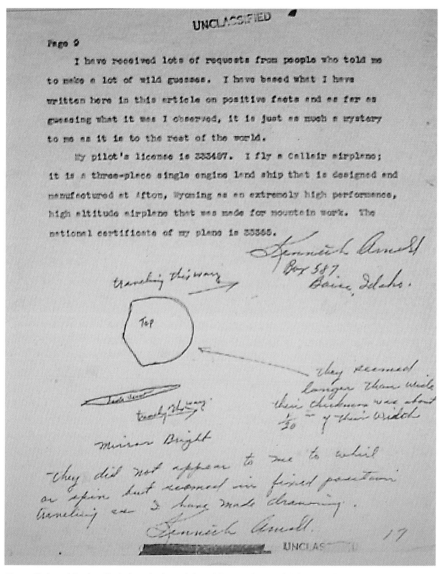

UNCLASSIFIED

Page 9

    I have received lots of requests from people who told me to make a lot of wild guesses. I have based what I have written here in this article on positive facts and as far as guessing what it was I observed, it is just as much a mystery to me as it is to the rest of the world.

    My pilot's license is 333487. I fly a Callair airplane; it is a three-place single engine land ship that is designed and manufactured at Afton, Wyoming as an extremely high performance, high altitude airplane that was made for mountain work. The national certificate of my plane is 33355.

Kenneth Arnold's detailed description of the objects along with his hand sketch.

search for a recently missing C46 transport aircraft of the US Air Force, which had offered a reward of $5,000.

In his spare time, Arnold was a member of the Idaho Search and Rescue Team and now and then earned a few dollars when a plane sometimes went missing in the mountains. Ground rescue teams estimated that the crash site of the Air Force plane was in the hard-to-reach Mount Rainier massif. Since the mountain chain was on his route anyway, Arnold decided to spend at least one hour searching. He took

Kenneth Arnold said: "They were flat like a frying pan and so smooth that they reflected the sun like a mirror."

off in Chehalis at around 2:00 p.m., reaching the area around Mount Rainier about one hour later. As Arnold scanned the slopes and the high plateau for the crashed transport plane, he was suddenly blinded by a light beam coming from the side. Arnold was shocked at first and assumed he was on a collision course with another aircraft. But there was no other plane to be seen far and wide. To be safe, Arnold looked again in all directions—then, suddenly, there it was again, this flash. Only then did Arnold see a formation of bright objects coming from the direction of Mount Baker at an unbelievable speed. By his own account, Arnold was around 120 miles (200 km) away from the objects. Thus, too far to be able to obtain accurate information about their size and shape. The only thing he could recognize was that they flew right towards Mount Rainier and were traveling in a sort of wedge-shaped

line. At first, Arnold took the strange formation to be a squad of Air Force jet aircraft, which were just on a training flight—but when he could not make out either wings, empennage, or position lights, he began to doubt his theory. The objects were flat, not quite round, and a bright blue-white light shone from their tops.

Only then did the businessman think of a secret type of Air Force aircraft—after all, as a skilled pilot, he had already seen all sorts of craft flying in the sky—but what he saw there in front of his eyes went far beyond his imagination. Never before had he been able to watch airplanes with these capabilities—as they were flying away, easily, like leaves in the wind and yet at an insane speed. As Kenneth Arnold glanced at his watch, it was exactly 2:59 p.m. He saw that the first object appeared to be just at the southern end of the mountain ridge, as the last of the group reached the northern one. This means that the formation of objects had to be at least five miles (eight km) long. In one minute, therefore, the fleet had traveled a distance of nearly fifty miles (eighty km) at a rate of around 2,050 mph (3,300 km/h)!

The entire strange spectacle had lasted only three minutes. Later, Arnold reported the incident to the authorities, and soon the press got wind of the story. At a hastily called press conference, the amateur pilot described his sighting in the following words:

> They were flat like a frying pan and so smooth that they reflected the sun like a mirror. You can call me an Einstein, a Flash Gordon, or simply call me a crackpot. But I know what I saw. Those things were flying like saucers when you skip them over water.

The next day, the local press reported: "Flying saucers over Mount Rainier"—and the headline soon went around the world. Suddenly, a new, and a modern myth was born, but at the same time a legend for the just dawning nuclear age. Had aliens visited the Earth on this said Tuesday in 1947, concerned people around the world all wondered at once. Where do they come from? What do they want?

Soon skeptics and scientists and UFO researchers countered with the question of whether these mysterious flying machines had really come from another world at all, or whether they in the end were indeed terrestrially produced craft. All over the world, experts and scientists ever-more intensely discussed these strange objects that had suddenly appeared out of nowhere. They were described by all strata of society, from ordinary workers, to police officers, to prominent persons from politics and economics. It has not been possible to resolve the mystery of the objects over Mount Rainier satisfactorily up till today. Neither the local authorities nor the FBI or other intelligence agencies have come to a final conclusion. Kenneth Arnold described the

Towards the end of World War II, Horten developed a flying wing design under the name Ho 229, equipped with a Jumo 004 jet engine, which reportedly could reach a top speed of about 621 mph (1,000 km/h).

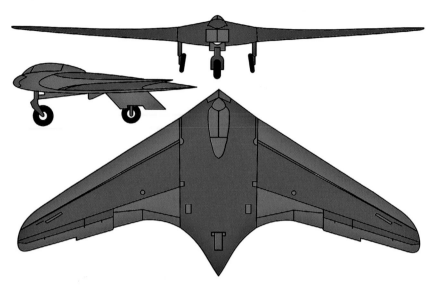

Simple outline drawing of Ho 229. Was Kenneth Arnold's sighting perhaps of an Ho 229, developed by the Horten brothers, in American possession?

objects as flat, crescent-shaped, and consisting of only one wing. Because this vague description— after all, he made the sighting at a distance of more than 124 miles (200 km), and was also dazzled by the sun—there was soon speculation about whether the objects could possibly be the Horten flying wing Ho 229 aircraft, because there would have been a parallel in time. The Horten Ho 229, developed towards the end of World War II, was a concept of Horten brothers and, like all Horten aircraft, involved flying wing design. Equipped with Junkers Jumo 004 jet engines, the craft were supposed to achieve a top speed of about 621 mph (1,000 km/h). It remains questionable, however, whether there ever really were test flights on German soil, because there are no corresponding documents or evidence for this. However, there is verified evidence that, after the end of World War II, parts of the Ho

229, such as the fuselage, were produced by the US Army in the United States, where they were probably further developed and also finished. Were there test flights of the Ho 229 conducted over Mount Rainier on June 24, 1947? Were these the mysterious objects that Kenneth Arnold saw? If these actually were a test flight of the Ho 229, a release of the records would be long overdue and would at least provide clarity in a case of a UFO sighting.

That UFOs, alternate reports by self-styled UFO researchers notwithstanding, are no phantasms is already shown just by the reaction of the Pentagon, which has always been quick to look for answers to the question of what could be behind the sightings of unidentified flying objects, and above all has always asked a crucial question: Are these objects a threat to the United States?

To find as precise an answer to this question as possible, "Project SIGN" was launched on January 22, 1948. The headquarters of the Commission of Inquiry was set up at Wright Patterson Air Force base. Here the threads were drawn together; here all the sightings were logged and investigated in detail—every small lead was examined. Here, none of those present from the Commission were satisfied with incomplete answers. Ultimately, no one responsible should be able to make the accusation that the investigations were run sloppily or even superficially. What mattered in the end were hard-hitting facts and results. During the thirteen months of work, SIGN investigated 240 domestic and thirty foreign cases. The results were astonishing: thirty percent of recorded sightings were based on illusion, natural phenomena, or confusion with conventional aircraft. By far the greater number, namely seventy percent, remain today unexplainable and unresolved. The term born of Kenneth Arnold's sighting of a "flying saucer" could, however, be regarded as impossible. It seemed too ridiculous to all parties, and it would not sufficiently take account of the seriousness of this project. So they decided on the simple and quite objective concept of an Unidentified Flying Object—UFO for short. Everyone from the Commission was soon clear about one fact: It was impossible to dismiss sightings of unidentified flying objects as pure nonsense or as imagination. Neither the Commission nor the Pentagon succeeded in doing this—because in any case, the many collected cases also included observations of senior military personnel, police officers, scientists, pilots, and politicians. Were they all supposed to be just crackpots or attention-seeking eyewitnesses?

Attention was paid to their statements about what they saw; ultimately, they indeed represented a certain position in society. There must, therefore, be something to the UFO sightings.

SIGN staff agreed towards the end of the 1940s that: It is possible that UFOs may involve alien spacecraft that visited the Earth because of the atom bomb tests.
(Department of Energy)

In the end, only one question remained open and kept presenting itself to the SIGN staff: Where did the objects come from? From the at-that-time hostile Soviet Union or from outer space? And though nothing could be conclusively explained, already one year later, in February 1949, the SIGN case files were closed again. A kind of final report, classified SECRET, noted: "It is possible that UFOs may involve alien spacecraft that visited the Earth because of the atom bomb tests. The assumption of this thesis was at least obvious—that in any case, for a long time, the greater number of United States' military installations were under temporary observation by unidentified flying objects, including the White Sands, New Mexico, missile test site. There was airtight evidence for this, because the test center

Open air museum in White Sands, New Mexico.

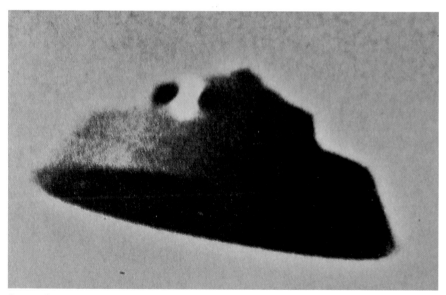

Among the contents of the GRUDGE project was to have every pilot immediately film any unknown object. Official US Air Force recording by a Douglas C47 pilot in July 1966 in Idaho.

at White Sands was equipped with all necessary devices for visual tracking of the missiles stationed there, so that it was possible to observe on the recorded footage of strange lights or objects from time to time over the test site.

At the same time, camera stations were installed over several square miles, which filmed a brisk UFO activity around the testing site and never ceased to amaze the personnel present. For a long time, a spy attack from the Soviet

This shot in the morning mist was reportedly taken by a US Navy pilot. A rugby-ball-shaped object flew over the aircraft carrier USS Kennedy.

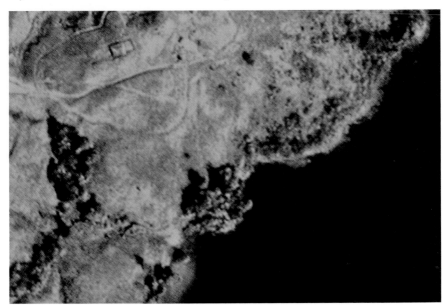

Random shot of an unknown dish-shaped object above Lago de Cote, Costa Rica, taken in 1971, for cartographic purposes. Computer analysis proves that this is a real physical object. (Geography Institute of Costa Rica)

Union was suspected, but then this thesis was rejected: Just how was the Soviet Union able to build aircraft with such exceptional flight characteristics? The objects sighted and filmed often meandered for hours above the facilities, then suddenly they were gone again, to re-emerge in the next moment somewhere else. The US intelligence agencies and military were under constant pressure during this period—they just had to find out where those strange objects came from. Project SIGN was officially abandoned, but in reality, it was internally renamed Project GRUDGE on February 11, 1949. Only the investigative strategy had changed: The aim was now to officially state that UFOs do not exist and attribute any detailed report of an unidentified flying object to pure fraud, psychosis, or in harmless cases, to confusion with balloons or aircraft. But the members of the committee were themselves soon quite clear about the fact that the many UFO sightings could not be thus so easily down-played or even swept under the carpet. There were simply too many new cases of sightings reported from across the country—and in many cases, the witnesses named in turn included respected citizens of the country. What was to be done? The US government was not only dealing with a practically unsolvable puzzle, but also facing the question of how they should behave without making themselves implausible or even ridiculous in public. Soon after, the intelligence services and military launched a new national campaign to, at least initially, finally get answers to the unanswered questions. From now on, cameras were installed in all US Air Force planes, and every pilot was ordered to immediately film any unfamiliar object. In addition, each pilot was handed an envelope with the inscription, "To be opened only in case of UFO sighting," containing further instructions on what actions the crew should take in the event of a UFO sighting. Project GRUDGE was renamed

again on March 16, 1952, as Project BLUE BOOK, and the experienced intelligence officer Edward J. Ruppelt was assigned to it, with astronomical adviser J. Allen Hynek, director of the McMillin Observatory of Ohio State University, at his side. Just two years later, Ruppelt and Hynek presented their Special Report No. 14, which documented a total of 3,200 sightings. The cases of sightings were classified as "known," "unknown," and "insufficient"—moreover, the quality of the reports was classified on a scale of one to four. The report classified sixty-nine percent of the cases as known and twenty-two percent as unknown. Some nine percent lacked further details. Some thirty-five percent of all so-called excellent cases were unknown, compared with only eighteen percent of the worst cases. Sightings of particularly trustworthy persons like policemen or army personnel were considered excellent cases.

Despite these circumstances, the US Air Force report was called into question, and it was claimed that none of the cited cases could even begin to provide proof that the objects observed involved extraterrestrial spacecraft. Edward J. Ruppelt was ultimately disappointed with the government's assessment of his work and criticized the evaluation in his book, *Report on Unidentified Flying Objects*, published in 1956. In his statements, Ruppelt even went a step further and gave as his opinion that the report has been misused for political purposes, also without the content being grasped in greater detail. J. Allen Hynek expressed the same view in his book, *The UFO Experience*, published in 1972, in which he incorporated not only experiences from Project BLUE BOOK, abandoned in 1969, but at the same time included a summary of Projects SIGN and GRUDGE. Hynek was of the opinion that the US Air Force was constantly striving to deceive the public about the reality and extent of the UFO phenomenon. The Project

BLUE BOOK files have been stored in the National Archives following the Freedom of Information Act and the contents have been made freely available to the public, but the names of all witnesses are unrecognizable and the report contains a public statement stating that none of the cases investigated could provide evidence of any extraterrestrial craft.

Strange celestial phenomena and the idea that these could be explained by visitors from an alien civilization, have always fascinated people at all times and in all epochs, but at the same time terrorized and frightened them. This was especially evident in 1938, when Orson Welles' production of *The War of the Worlds* went on the air. This extremely realistic radio play, produced like a normal music entertainment program, with news, numerous program breaks, and apparent live hook-ups with live on-site reports, sparked outright mass panic among the population in New Jersey. Of course, the broadcast date also contributed a great deal to this. It was October 30, 1938, the eve of the traditional Halloween holiday and on the eve of World War II. Fear and uncertainty were already, so to speak, heavy in the air—and many listeners missed the preliminary announcement that this was merely a harmless radio play. They heard the alleged CBS live reportage from the Martians had supposedly landed on a site in New Jersey. Here is an excerpt:

> I see two luminous disks that are peering out of a hole . . . could they be eyes? Or is that a face? It might . . . good heavens, something is winding out of the shadows, like a gray snake. Now even a second . . . and another . . . and another . . . Now I can see the body of the thing . . . It . . . ladies and gentlemen . . . is indescribable. I can hardly look at it, it's so awful!

J. Allan Hynek, shown here, headed Project BLUE BOOK jointly with Edward J. Ruppelt.

Alleged comments from astronomers on the (of course fictitious) imposition of a state and statements of the (also fictional) Secretary of the Interior gave the whole thing a definite official character. A later investigation ultimately revealed that at least one-fifth of the approximately six million known listeners believed what they heard on the radio. But there was worse to come: The play sparked veritable mass panic among the population. People tried to escape the Martian invasion, barricaded themselves in their homes, thousands warned their family members in the area by telephone and tried to escape inland by car—just far enough away to get out "from the hell of New Jersey." Orson Welles' radio play showed in a real and dramatic way how people would react to an extraterrestrial landing. Thus we assume that the population would say of every UFO sighting that it involves visitors from an intelligence still foreign to us, so this could

A radio play by Orson Welles showed that extraterrestrial visitors would probably trigger a panic among the population. This artistic representation is one of the countless impressions of an alien "invasion."

definitely again lead to a mass panic among the population. That at least is suggested by scientists and politicians around the world. Is this the grounds for the governmental and military strategy to dismiss reports of sightings of unidentified flying objects as pure fraud or hallucination?

4. UFOs Over the Soviet Union

September 20, 1977. Early risers among the 185,000 inhabitants of the Karelian capital city of Petrozavodsk, in the former Soviet Union, could not believe their eyes this Tuesday when they looked at the night sky at four o'clock in the morning and suddenly saw a bright star flash out. It had been raining all night, now the rain had finally stopped, and the earlier almost total cloud cover thinned somewhat, so the stars could be seen every now and again between individual wispy clouds. One star kept coming closer and descended in a kind of spiral path. Soon after, it transformed itself into a fiery ball and remained stationary for about seven minutes over the city. Just at this moment, a sound penetrated the morning silence like the wail of a siren. But as suddenly as the howling began, it stopped again, and the light phenomenon now began moving, silently, and appearing like a red-orange hemisphere over Petrosavodsk. Eyewitnesses later reported that they saw a light in the inner half of the hemisphere that was pulsing at a frequency of approximately 2 Hz and became alternately brighter and darker. Meanwhile, a telescope-like beam of light now slid perpendicularly from under the object to the ground; a second followed the first, weaker and briefer. After some time, both disappeared; now many small, thin, blue-white brilliant beams appeared instead at the edge of the object in a kind of jagged structure that seemed literally to rain on the ground. After a few seconds, the object's color changed from blue to gold, and it looked as if thousands of thin needles were pelting the earth in a downpour. The eerie light apparition now looked like a jellyfish with golden tentacles.

The white zone around the hemisphere had meanwhile pulled together into a glowing ring and the beams appeared slightly curved. But the high point of the sighting was yet to come. When the light spectacle was over, many eager onlookers discovered that the falling golden needles had burned holes in the asphalt, in the windows of a factory building, or even in walls of houses. Meanwhile, the object had moved on and was poised above an eighty-eighty-mile (142 meter) long ship, which was moored in the city harbor—in comparison with it, the object's size could be estimated at around sixty-five miles (104 meters). Later, eyewitnesses reported in interviews that the object shone so brightly that their eyes hurt when they looked at it directly—but strangely enough, the witnesses did not have the impression that the surrounding environment was illuminated at the same time.

Investigations on the ground revealed that, at the time of the sighting, many people were woken from sleep and had complained of feeling unwell. Many felt a form of depression, others had nightmares or reported "inner surges of electricity." Other eyewitnesses in turn stood in front of the windows of their apartments, as if in shock and shouted out loud or ran in panic in the streets, shouting: "This is the end." By that time, the object was still visible in the whole city, since it was positioned directly above the harbor. Meanwhile, another smaller object detached itself from the bright body, which was described by several eyewitnesses as a fiery discus, which later reportedly flew back to the big object.

A doctor was among the witnesses, who had stopped straight on his way to a patient—virtually

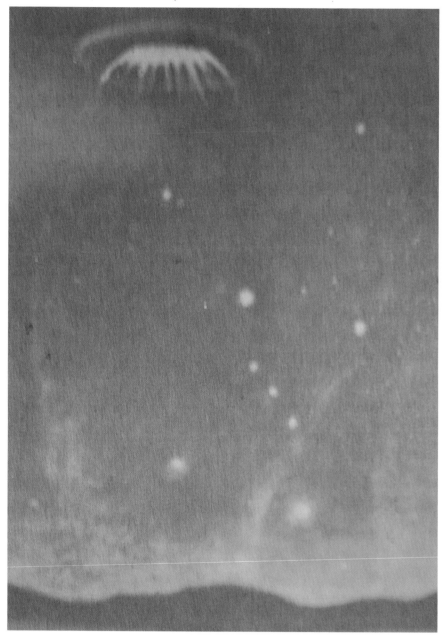

On the night of September 20, 1977, at 4:00 a.m., thousands of people in the Karelian capital Petrozavodsk saw a light phenomenon that appeared "like a jellyfish of light, shining in glorious colors, with golden tentacles." (Schwede archive}

Drawing of the Petrosavodsk UFO, based on eyewitness information, in the US tabloid National Enquirer.

at the same time, the entire computer system of an institute for data processing shut down.

There were tumultuous scenes in the streets of Petrozavodsk, according to the police. Many people, including some later eyewitnesses, gave the impression of being mentally disturbed or sensed a feeling of depression—at the same time, these people believed to smell ozone in the air they breathed. Finally, after several minutes, the rain of beams stopped and the brightness around the object decreased significantly. But the astonished people still directed their eyes anxiously to the sky, and they stared as if electrified at the uncanny object that now suddenly threatened to crash, but seemed to take hold of itself moments later and again ascended, to then quickly fly away towards Lake Onega with a bright reddish tail behind it. The hemisphere broke through a dark bank of clouds, in which burned a bright red ring, coloring the clouds violet at the top and light green to white at the bottom. For a long time, many red semicircles were still clearly visible inside this cloud, and one last time, two long beams of light shot down to earth from the hole—only the object itself could no longer be seen.

In the days that followed, some local newspapers cited numerous Soviet scientists, including the director of the local observatory, V. Krat, who were all of the opinion that what had been seen at Petrozavodsk was simply the launch of the Cosmos 955 satellite, which took place at 4:03 a.m. (Moscow time) in Plesetsk, 186 miles (300 km) away. This theory soon generated headlines all over the country and even brought Russian news agency Tass correspondent Nicolai Milov to the scene. But Milov did not believe the rocket launch story and made his way to the scene of the incident to get a picture himself of everything that had really happened there in the early morning hours of September 20. During several months, he questioned over a hundred eyewitnesses, who could not all believe that this spectacle could only be a matter of a rocket launch; in the end, people in this region were very familiar with rocket launches. For a long time nothing happened; not a single article by Milov appeared in any newspaper in the country during the following months—only about one year after the incident did the state central organizations Pravda and Izvestia finally report in detail about the events in Petrozavodsk. Only now did it become known that the object had already been sighted hours before the alleged rocket launch and the appearance in Petrozavodsk had been sighted in many other parts of the country. On the evening before, at around 6:00 p.m., eyewitnesses in the province of Sverdlovsk, about 124 miles (200 km) north of Petrozavodsk, saw a glowing red body, with a dozen or so powerful beams of light raining down to the earth from underneath it. The object was about the size of the full moon, according to witness reports. Here also, a few minutes later, something not described any more specifically than as a smaller flying body, separated itself from the big object, flew away, and turned "into a jellyfish"—like the object described in Petrozavodsk. After about five minutes, the phenomenon moved towards Surgut and finally disappeared over the horizon.

The object was also observed simultaneously in Demyanka, located thirty-one miles (fifty km) west of Lake Ilmen, as a phenomenon glowing bright red. Eyewitnesses claimed to have spotted a second small object. Thus, all the facts suggest that these light phenomena could well involve the object from Petrozavodsk—especially since the track of the "light jellyfish" could be followed even further. It was about 3:00 a.m., when the writer Limik finished his last corrections to a short story in the small town of Namoyev, located around twenty-two miles (thirty-five km) northwest of Petrozavodsk. Limik was used to working at night because he had peace; everything around was quiet and finally, for him, the night had something magical about it. After doing his work, Limik went to the door to get some more fresh air just before going to bed. Suddenly his interest was aroused by a strange reddish light on the horizon. Curious, Limik wanted to get to the bottom of the matter and got a telescope out of the house to see the strange light better. Only now did he see that it was a glowing ring, surrounded by a semi-transparent purple glowing lenticular object. Limik was fascinated; he had never seen anything like it in his life. He was able to watch the lights in the morning sky for a good fifteen minutes. An eerie spectacle, as Limik will testify later, because after some time, bright pulsating light beams, like tentacles, also emerged from several openings in the object. Limik watched how the object eventually flew away in a northerly direction and at the same time heard all the dogs in the neighborhood howling. About an hour later, around 4:00 a.m., many fishermen in Lomonosov, on the southern shore of the Gulf of Finland, observed a similar radiant light jellyfish, from which a small orange glowing ball descended and then flew away eastwards. Did these cases all involve one and the same object? If so, this would be certain evidence that the sighting in Petrozavodsk could

Night rocket launch over Florida, taken several miles/kilometers from the launch site. Many scientists today hold the view that the light phenomenon over Petrozavodsk was caused by the simultaneous launch of the Cosmos 995 spy satellite from Plesetsk, 186 miles (300 km) east of Petrozavodsk. (Shutterstock)

not possibly be the Cosmos 955 satellite. But not only the light phenomenon itself puzzled researchers; the "needle shower," the many holes left in the asphalt and windowpanes, also posed a number of outstanding issues to all of science. A research team even traveled from distant Hawaii to Moscow to study glass samples from the perforated windows from Petrozavodsk at the Academy of Sciences; they found that it was as if many of the approximately quarter-inch (five to seven mm)-sized holes had melted into the glass in nearly rectangular shapes, and crystalline structures were discovered on the cut surfaces under an electron microscope for which no logical explanation has been found so far. Ultimately, the case forced all established science in the Soviet Union to deal with it, and the President of the Academy of Sciences, W. Migulin, even convened its own commission of inquiry, which, however, never came to any conclusive results in the course of their work regarding what really happened over the Karelian capital in those morning hours of September 20, 1977. For the record, Migulin only acknowledged, in a briefly formulated press statement, that the light phenomenon could be traced back either to a natural atmospheric phenomenon or to the launch of the Cosmos 995 satellite in Plesetsk, 186 miles (300 km) east of Petrozavodsk.

Soon, however, Migulin realized that the thesis about the satellite launch was on shaky ground, and could not explain any of the occurrences, such as the holes in windows, asphalt, and building walls. In the Soviet newspaper *The Week*, Migulin soon after apologized for his inadequate investigative results and acknowledged that the history of science had provided virtually no scientific expertise about the event in Petrozavodsk which could contribute to a solution. And about forty years later, the case remains mysterious. It is not rare that unidentified flying objects leave behind such distinct traces. But most investigations of the traces, as in Petrozavodsk, do not lead to any conclusive results, but rather to an even greater number of further questions—as in the next case as well, which also occurred in the former Soviet Union.

October 29, 1986, a Wednesday: Two girls from Dalnegorsk, near the city of Vladivostok, at around 7:55 p.m., saw a red glowing sphere, which was flying horizontally, almost silently from the southwest, towards the more than 2,000-foot (611 meter) high Isvestkovaya Mountain. Suddenly, the sphere changed its trajectory and crashed into the mountain, tearing out a large rock. The girls and several other eyewitnesses standing around heard a deafening thud shortly after the impact. Soon after, the eyewitnesses saw that the sphere appeared to be attempting several times to rise up again, but could not do so. With each renewed attempt, it glowed bright red and sent strange rays to the ground. After half an hour, as the sphere failed to fly on after some six attempts to rise, it apparently destroyed itself and flared up as bright as a welding torch. The sphere blazed for an hour, until there was nothing left except a large number of metal pellets and ash residue. Scientists studied the crash site for two days and established that the slate was burned black and cracked to a depth of approximately nearly fifty feet (fifteen meters), and that the strange metal pellets, which consisted primarily of lead, contained a peculiar substance: fine, net-like, brittle, and mixed with glass. The substance has been studied in three research centers, and eleven research institutes, which resulted in a precise spectral analysis that showed that the pellets also contained, in addition to lead, twenty percent silicon, ten percent aluminum, fifteen percent iron, one and one-half percent zinc, two percent titanium, one percent magnesium, two percent silver, and trace amounts of copper, calcium, vanadium, chromium, cerium, nickel, cobalt, lanthanum, molybdenum, and sodium. The researchers found, however, no conclusive explanation for the web-like substance. An expert on carbon at the Chemical Institute of Vladivostok, stated:

It is impossible to understand what this is. It is reminiscent of glassy carbon. The conditions under which it is formed, are unknown. It is possible that extremely high temperatures could produce it.

Under the microscope, they also found quartz threads with a thickness of seventeen microns on many pieces of this fibrous substance. In comparison, most human hair has a thickness of fifty-six micrometers. Some of these filaments consisted of a few dozen threads twirled together—and in one of these inward-twined threads, they found a thread made of gold. Chemists from Vladivostok, after completing their investigation, were in agreement that this certainly could only be a product of extraterrestrial origin. No earthly production process is able to make so fine a material. Further investigations at the crash site also showed increased radioactivity, whatever the cause for this might be, so that the team of scientists who had often stayed at the site for more than twenty-four hours during their investigations, complained of balance and cognitive disorders. In addition, changes in blood composition, and increased heart rate and blood pressure values were observed among the participants. Ornithologists also made a strange discovery: In a study conducted over some five years, they were able to show that there were no birds at the area in question around the crash site at the time in question. Soviet science was also confronted with a puzzle at this time, that

still has not been solved in any case. On the evening of November 28, 1987, the region at the crash site in Dalnegorsk was visited again. From 9:00 p.m. until well after midnight, people from Dalnegorsk right up the east coast towards Primorye, watched a veritable UFO invasion. Hundreds of eyewitnesses reported they saw a good dozen spheres, cylinders, and up to approximately 984-foot- (300 meter) long "cigars" in a radius of approximately a mile to a mile and one-half (two to three km) at low altitude around the crash site of the sphere. "They searched the entire area with huge headlights," or so the astonished witnesses told journalists, who had traveled there from across the country. Other witnesses reported power outages and cars whose engines suddenly turned off. In the years that followed, there were more unexplained UFO sightings reported in the entire region. Were the unknown objects perhaps looking for the crashed sphere, or are there perhaps special natural resources or minerals in that region, that could be of significant importance for the unknown visitors? These are questions without answers to this day, and even the enlightened science of current times, with modern technical means, cannot seem to solve the mysteries.

What is particularly striking about the UFO reports from the former Soviet Union, and today's Russia, is the normal way in which newspapers and news agencies from around the country report stories of this type. In German newspapers, even those which run sensational news or don't take their reports' veracity so seriously, UFO reports arouse nothing more than a tired smile; journalists who might look at such a story twice and research the reports meticulously and with due journalistic care, and make them into headlines, must ultimately fear for their reputations. In general, the view is always that UFOs can only be attributed to dreamers looking for an effect,

and no one who is even remotely in full possession of his mental faculties would put forth such tales in the world. No wonder then that many eyewitnesses who have observed something unusual in the sky don't want to see their names in the newspaper or in television broadcasts and only report off camera about what they really saw. Sometimes, however, these witnesses also have the courage to appear under their full name before journalists and running TV cameras to tell about their experiences—as the next chapter shows.

A "red glowing ball" crashed within the marked area on the more than 2,000-foot-(611 meter)-high Isvestkovaya Mountain on October 29, 1986, at about 7:55 p.m. and burned up completely. (Wikimedia)

5. UFO Sightings by Pilots

As explained at the end of the previous chapter, it is not easy to motivate eyewitnesses to talk about unusual sightings in the sky. There are two reasons: First, these people are concerned about their reputations, especially if they are working in a responsible position—often rightly so. Second, they may initially not be so clear about the fact that they have just become an eyewitness of something unusual. During my research, I have ascertained that a considerable number of witnesses had never before in their lives seriously dealt with UFOs, not to mention experiences with "aliens." That, in my opinion, puts the testimony of these witnesses in a different light. This group of people don't want to make themselves important; they don't want publicity—they simply just believe what they saw and stand by it. Pilots are undoubtedly among the most valuable eyewitness. Already

in 1954, there was a comparatively well-documented case, when the pilots and passengers of a BOAC Stratocruiser airliner, flying at cruising altitude on June 29 near Labrador, Canada, noticed one oblong object and several small ones. The objects were about four or five miles away and remained in sight about twenty minutes. A combat aircraft that took off in the wake of the sighting was unable to find the object, however. Captain James Howard and other members of the crew and passengers repeatedly confirmed their sightings to the press in the days and weeks after the flight.

In addition, the former Lufthansa chief pilot, Werner Utter, who died in November 2006, at the age of eighty-five, confirmed in numerous interviews that he had had repeated encounters with unidentified flying objects and that he had always remained silent about the incidents

A BOAC Boeing Stratocruiser. Captain James Howard was flying an aircraft of this type on June 29, 1954, over Labrador, when he noticed several objects a few miles away, which remained in sight for about twenty minutes. Other members of his crew and some passengers later testified to this. (Schwede Archive)

throughout his time of service, due to fear of being vilified or even ultimately losing his pilot's license. In 1980, Utter, aboard a Boeing 747-type cargo aircraft on a flight from New York to Frankfurt, at more than 39,000 feet (12,000 meters), had the following encounter with an unidentified flying object, which he describes in a conversation with the astrophysicist Illobrand von Ludwiger in the following words:

> We were just flying over England, when the flight engineer next to me shouted: "Watch out, there's something coming!" I looked out. Something that looked like a huge cigar was moving rapidly straight towards us. I couldn't do anything; the jumbo is flying at a speed of about 621 mph (1,000 kilometers per hour). At the last moment, this thing went away under the wing. We reported right away to the next radar control center, Maastricht Control, and asked if they had seen something, but there was nothing on the radar.

More than 4,000 UFO sightings by pilots have now been meticulously compiled and carefully analyzed by former NASA employee Dr. Richard Haines. The sightings by pilots alone may be an indication that encounters with UFOs are in no way based on figments of imagination or the fantasies of affected witnesses. Former pilot Jean-Charles Duboc of the French airline Air France, can also confirm this. Duboc recalls exactly his inexplicable encounter at nearly 33,000 feet (10,000 meters) in the air. It happened on Air France flight 3532 from Nice to London in January 1994:

> It seemed to be a huge flying disk. It stabilized and stopped moving. We watched the object for more than a minute to the left of our airplane. Surprisingly, it stood completely still in the sky, and then gradually disappeared. We knew nothing about the nature of UFOs; it seemed to be embedded in a kind of magnetic or gravitational field and had neither lights nor any other visible metallic structure. Therefore, it seemed really blurry. The most incredible thing was that it became transparent within ten to twenty seconds and then disappeared. At the same time, the radar of the Air Defense command center registered a point crossing our trajectory for one minute long. When I recorded the estimated position of the UFO on a flight map, I was surprised to realize that it had remained near the Taverny Base, where the French Strategic Air Command headquarters is located. This sighting was investigated by the COMETA Group of the French military, headed by Gen. Denis Letty, in cooperation with several senior French Defense officers with GEPAN (now GEIPAN, Groupe d'Étude des Phénomènes Aérospatiaux Non-identifiés) at the French space agency, CNES.

It was never possible to determine the real background; the Air France crew is clear about only one thing—that the case described was no hallucination. The following case also illustrates vividly that it is 99.9 percent clear that it could not have been an illusion or a purely atmospheric phenomenon. In this case, the eyewitnesses were the pilot of a Boeing 747 cargo plane of Japan Airlines (JAL) as well as his co-pilot and flight engineer. November 17, 1986—Flight JAL 1628 Paris to Tokyo is at about 33,000 feet (10,000 meters) over Alaska. It is 5:10 p.m.—at this latitude, it is pitch dark all day this time of

Kenju Terauchi has more than nineteen years of flying experience and has encountered a lot as a military pilot, but he found what he saw hard to put into words, by his own admission, on the night of the November 17, 1986.

year; only the full moon bathes the icy landscape far below in an inhospitable light. The weather is calm, and there are two crews working on board the Boeing cargo plane, who alternate with each other during the sixteen-hour flight, so that each of the crew members can sleep once for a few hours. Kenju Terauchi is in command on board—he has more than nineteen years of flying experience and already previously experienced a lot as a military pilot. Through all the years, Kenju Terauchi has made a resolution that he only believes in what he sees with his own eyes.

Nobody can fool him and his crew so easily. But what he and his crew experienced that night, they would not forget in their lifetimes. Terauchi, who was on numerous talk shows around the world after his experience, including on German television, recalls the events of that November evening very exactly, long after the incident:

It was about 05:10 p.m.—this strange phenomenon began during a left turn. Lights were moving directly in front of us, in the same direction, and at the same tempo as ours. After maybe six minutes, they suddenly jumped, in a fraction of less than one second, to another position. Then they were back right in front of us. In the light of the full moon, you could recognize their source as rectangles with jets from which white, amber lights were shooting, which pulsed in the direction of a dark, vertical field

Kenju Terauchi and his crew sighted the mysterious objects while aboard their Japanese airline JA Boeing 747 cargo plane. (Gilland)

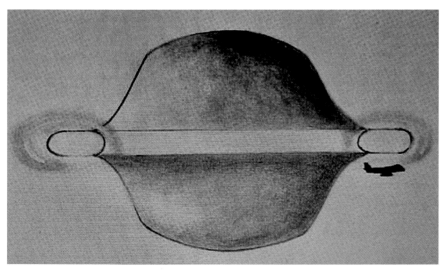

This sketch is intended to illustrate the relative sizes. The stylized Boeing 747 seems actually tiny compared to the giant UFO.

in the middle of each of the two objects. They were so close and so bright that the entire cockpit was brightly lit up.

Terauchi, his co-pilot Takanori Tamefuji, and flight engineer Yoshio Tsukuba had never seen anything so strange in their lives. It was immediately clear to Terauchi that what was in motion right in front of him, could not be of this world. It was not any aircraft known to him. He soon ruled out lightning or St. Elmo's fire. A dozen lights were shining out from the strange rectangular objects in red, green, white, and orange—the full range of spectral colors. Immediately, co-pilot Takanori Tamefuiji contacts the Air Route Traffic Control Center in Anchorage to find out whether any other aircraft are in Alaskan airspace. The ground control officer on duty said there were none and confirmed, after a second request, that he couldn't see a single object on his radar screen. The military air surveillance was also unable to log any air traffic in the specified corridor. The crew

was baffled, but Terauchi and his crew were sure that what they saw before their eyes was not imaginary but real. At this moment, the thought came to Terauchi for the first time that the objects could possibly be UFOs. He had often read and heard about such things—even among colleagues, one or the other had seen such things—but Terauchi never thought it possible that phenomena of this kind really exist. Could he also be the witness of such an event? Terauchi and his crew remained calm during the next few minutes, because at this point there was no reason to panic—which would change soon: "The two objects were 984 feet (300 meters) away from our Boeing and were the size of a DC8. We did not feel threatened by their maneuvers. On the contrary. Somehow, there was something calming coming from these objects." Then suddenly, the two objects disappeared again as fast as they had come. But as soon as the situation on board the Boeing had again somewhat normalized, suddenly there appeared behind the cargo plane

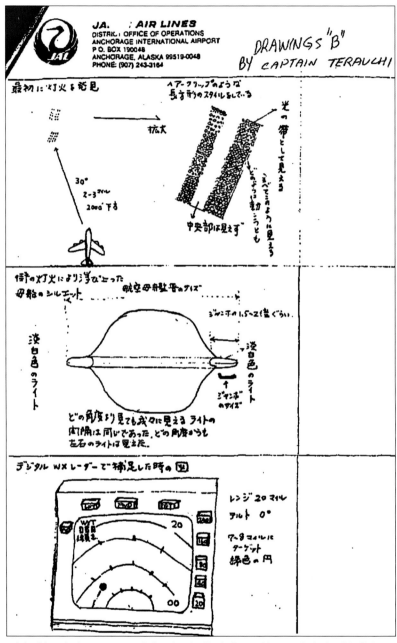

The original handwritten notes and sketches by Kenju Terauchi, recorded after his flight.

the gigantic outline of another object. At this moment, Terauchi and his crew sensed fear. The object was dangerously close and was the size of an aircraft carrier. Never before had Terauchi and his crew seen something so gigantic in the sky.

"We asked for change of course and turned left to escape from the spaceship—but in vain; when we looked out the window, it was still there. Finally, we asked permission to change our altitude and started a descent, but the ship continued to fly in formation with our Boeing. For the first time, a sense of dread overcame us all. Who were they and what were their intentions towards us?"

All civil and military radar stations around Alaska were instantly alerted. The Air Force proposed deploying fighter interceptors—but Terauchi and his crew rejected the proposal on the grounds that military intervention could provoke the unknown pursuers unnecessarily. Terauchi and his crew were followed by the spacecraft for more than forty minutes. Meanwhile, the Air Route Traffic Control Center had a United Airlines plane flying nearby on their radar screen and asked the crew for support; as it eventually appeared at the altitude of the Boeing cargo plane, the ship disappeared as suddenly as it had appeared from nowhere. Terauchi and his crew were speechless:

There was nothing more there. The thing was gone all at once; it followed us for as long as fifty minutes, and suddenly, it was no longer there.

At 6:25 p.m., JAL Flight 1628 landed safely at Anchorage Airport; in the meantime, the air traffic authority had even called up a crisis management team to advise on taking further steps in this matter. The entire crew was then medically examined, but no health-related abnormality could be detected in any of the crew members—all were at the time in a sound, medically flawless condition, so the crew soon continued their flight to Tokyo undisturbed.

What did Terauchi and his crew see aboard the cargo plane that night? Due to public interest, the case was handed over to the FAA (Federal Aviation Administration) on January 1, 1987, barely two months after the incident. But the briefly formulated FAA final report only states: "[…] was unable to confirm the event." The FAA was, therefore, according to its own statement, unable to confirm the incident described.

On the radar contacts, the report correspondingly states: The radar contacts were explained as uncorrelated primary and secondary contacts, in which the actual position of an aircraft (primary contact) and that of the Air Traffic Control transponder (secondary contact) are not synchronized and on this stated grounds, two targets are displayed on the radar screen.

On the crew's descriptions of the objects, the FAA stated concisely: "It is impossible for us to investigate possible UFO sightings of crew members on board an aircraft." The Committee for Skeptical Inquiry (CSI), an internationally active group of scientific skepticism organization founded in the United States by the philosopher Paul Kurtz in 1976, published the following statement on the events of November 17, 1986, under the direction of Philip J. Klass:

The sighting of the first two luminous objects only involved a matter of ice crystals, which were reflected by the light of the full moon shining on the evening in question. After the Boeing had passed the ice crystals, the crew searched for the supposedly disappeared UFO and thus discovered the planet Venus. This was then taken for the huge UFO. The radar contacts are merely due to thin cloud banks.

So was it just an illusion? Hardly, contends physicist Bruce Maccabee. Both the FAA paper and the CSI declaration show significant deficiencies, in his opinion. According to Maccabee's view, both investigative reports simply ignore several of the points described. There is the described shape of the objects, further sense impressions, and especially the objects' pattern of movement. The FAA radar analysis does not agree with Maccabee on any of the noted points, so he ultimately concluded that the incident will probably remain forever unexplained. This would also confirm the thesis of John Callahan. Callahan, who headed the Department of Accidents and Investigations for the FAA from 1981 to 1988, confirmed only many years after his retirement, that all the data on the case were collected and extensively discussed at a joint ninety-minute meeting of CIA staff and the US President's Scientific Advisory Staff, which Callahan personally attended. The unanimous conclusion was that the available evidence, including the thirty-minute radar recording, would indicate a UFO and that the radar recordings did not involve either an initially presumed hardware failure or a software failure. The CIA also investigated the incident and confiscated all compiled data and witness statements. After the investigations, John Callahan presented the event along with the final report to the science staff of former President Ronald Reagan. His suggestion that they publish the report and confirm the authenticity of the case met with severe criticism from the CIA, which was of the opinion that publishing the report could cause panic in the population. Callahan remembers the exact words at the end of the meeting: "When we finished, someone from the CIA said: 'This meeting never took place. We were never here, you are all sworn to secrecy, and we are confiscating all this data.'" Now Callahan was also firmly convinced that the entire FAA analysis of the radar data was intentionally manipulated to downplay the seriousness of the incident. According to the National Aviation Reporting Center on Anomalous Phenomena (NARCAP), some 3,500 sightings of unidentified flying objects and phenomena by military, commercial, and civilian pilots have since been documented. But Jim Courant, a flight captain for thirty-one years, believes that the number is likely to be much higher and thinks that it is the case that encounters between civil and military aircraft and unidentified flying objects are not often reported. Jim Courant has been concerned with the UFO phenomenon for more than ten years, and his library now includes more than 3,000 titles on this subject; for three years, he was also host of the television series *New Perspectives*—he still works full-time as a commercial pilot. Due to the now wide awareness of his name, he has met over the years with many military and civilian pilots, who repeatedly reported to him about encounters with unknown phenomena and objects and about how difficult it was for them to go public with them. Jim Courant stated, during the Citizen Hearing on Disclosure, on the facts about the existence of extraterrestrials on Earth at the National Press Club in Washington, DC, on May 3, 2013:

These pilots are afraid. Not because of their status or because of the risk of reprisals against them. No, rather they fear for their families.

Former Apollo 14 astronaut Edgar Dean Mitchell does not believe that man is alone in the universe and has been fighting for years for the US government to reconsider its policy of confidentiality on alleged UFO incidents. (NASA)

Jim Courant recalls an incident that had occurred in 1980, over the Pacific as an unidentified flying object suddenly appeared before the eyes of the crew of a Boeing 747, which was more than twice the size of the jumbo jet. The Boeing pilot reported to Courant later in a detailed conversation about how much pressure he and his crew had been put under after landing in Japan, to not speak to anyone about this incident. Courant recalled a separate incident in this context, which took place near Albuquerque, New Mexico, in 1995: "The object suddenly shot upwards in a flash of garish white light at a forty-five-degree angle. Four other pilots saw the unknown object also. One of the pilots said later that it could have been a meteor. I replied: 'Since when do meteors fly backwards?'" Courant is confident that commercial pilots in particular, who often fly for hours at more than 32,000 feet (10,000 meters) in the air, have seen a whole range of objects that suddenly appear from nowhere and sometimes move forward at speeds that cannot be achieved with today's state-of-the-art technologies; you also cannot, according to Courant, dismiss all the pilot reports of UFO sightings as just crazy ideas. Courant says: "Pilots take their profession very seriously and are rarely prone to exaggeration." During the hearing, Jim Courant was convinced by the fact that when it comes to information, there is still much to be done in the field of UFO research and called for the US government to finally inform the public on this issue and the information they had assembled during many years of research. Courant added: "UFO sightings are just the tip of the iceberg when you consider what has been discovered and what is really known about aliens." This was confirmed by former Apollo 14 astronaut Edgar Dean Mitchell. Mitchell called upon the Obama administration to finally end the secrecy about UFOs. According to him, the government knows far more than they admit

and is doing everything to keep it secret from the population. At a press conference at the National Press Club in Washington, DC, following the 2009 X-Conference, which was broadcast by CNN and many other television stations, Mitchell expressed himself in the following words:

It is time to end the truth embargo on extraterrestrial presence. I, therefore, call on our government to open up. Other governments, such as of Belgium, France, Brazil, Argentina, and Mexico have already released their documents. We should now do the same thing and connect ourselves to this planetary community, which is present, to take up their proper place as a space-faring civilization.

Dean Mitchell grew up in Roswell, New Mexico—thus, in the city where many UFO adherents are convinced that a UFO with aliens on board reportedly crashed in 1947. The former Apollo 14 astronaut has dealt extensively with the events of that time in the past, has interviewed still-surviving former eyewitnesses, and gone in search of clues on the ground. His conclusion: The US military has done everything in due course to cover up the crash, and the military has allegedly intimidated witnesses to silence them, as Mitchell commented on CNN. In the course of his research, Mitchell encountered a number of eyewitnesses who were already advanced in years, but could still remember that event in 1947 exactly. Everyone had so much explosive material that Mitchell considered himself obligated to appear in person at the Pentagon on this matter, with a request that the truth finally be made public after more than sixty years. And indeed, an unnamed admiral turned to him and promised to find out the truth and confirmed, at least in essential respects, the accuracy of those witnesses' information. But

NASA also has countless shots of unidentified objects in their archives. This image is reportedly a satellite photo. The origin of the object is unknown. (NASA)

when the admiral attempted to find out more details about the crash, he was stopped by the highest authorities and thereupon disavowed the instructions about the just recently confirmed information about an alleged UFO crash in Roswell. Mitchell was then visibly irritated, but affirmed: "What happened in Roswell on July 5, 1947, is the truth. My friends, who at the time witnessed the events with their own eyes and are now long since dead, told me the truth. A governmental organization to maintain secrecy about these incidents is working even today to successfully cover up this important event in the history of mankind."

6. The Roswell File

What exactly happened in July 1947 near the small desert town of Roswell, New Mexico? UFO skeptics and advocates have repeatedly kept clashing fiercely on this issue. Ever since the publication of the book by Charles Berlitz and William Moore, *The Roswell Incident—The UFOs and the CIA,* in 1980, Roswell was suddenly on everyone's lips. The authors wrote in their work about a crashed UFO and alien creatures that were reportedly found next to the wreck. In the following years, a number of books and films by various authors were published on the subject, and soon the putative UFO crash in Roswell became the best-known UFO event in the world. But the question of what really happened there remains unanswered to this day—at least by the government. On June 14, 1947, rancher William Brazel found some strange debris, its origin he could not explain, on the Foster Ranch, approximately 65 miles (105 km) northwest of Roswell. Brazel decided to take some of the parts home. In early July, the rancher finally learned that several unidentified flying objects had been spotted in the area and that one of the objects reportedly crashed in the desert. Brazel immediately sat up and took notice, recalling the strange parts that he had found a month earlier and stored in a shed. Could they perhaps come from the object that supposedly crashed? Brazel did not take long to think about it, and immediately informed the sheriff of Chaves County, George Wilcox, about his strange find. Wilcox inspected

Roswell Army Air Force base in 1947. This is where the wreckage of the crashed UFOs were first found.

General Ramey and Col. Roger Duboise show journalists the wreckage, which, depending upon interpretation, came from a crashed UFO—or a weather balloon.

Major Jesse A. Marcel shows more wreckage to journalists and photographers in General Ramey's office during another press conference.

the parts and immediately realized that this matter was something too big for him. The sheriff informed the Roswell Air Force base. Subsequently, the area around the site where the debris was discovered was widely cordoned off, and since the Army staff were also unable to explain the exact origin of the parts, all the material was handed over for further analysis to the Army base in Fort Worth, Texas.

Meanwhile, the press had gotten wind of the matter. The next day, the *Roswell Daily Record* ran the following headline:

The news about a supposedly crashed UFO spread like wildfire around the globe. Here is the headline of the Roswell Daily Record *of July 8, 1947.*

The many rumors about flying disks became reality yesterday, since an intelligence officer of the 509th Bomb Group of Roswell Air Force Base was lucky enough to take custody of one of these disks.

The news struck like a bombshell. Could aliens really have landed on Earth? Roswell was on everyone's lips; the message spread like wildfire—right around the globe. Suddenly, people all over the world were discussing the fact that we probably are not alone in the universe. The man responsible for this report was Walter G. Haut, press officer at the Air Force base in Roswell. Meanwhile, of course, the Pentagon and the CIA had learned of the strange finds and decided that they could not shock the world public with such a report. Within twenty-four hours, the report had been denied from the

Is this the crashed disk of Roswell? The information on the shape and size vary, depending on the source.

A Mogul weather balloon. The debris from one such as this was allegedly found on Mac Brazel's ranch. (USAF)

highest levels. Now there was no longer talk of a "flying saucer"; rather it was now said that the salvaged parts were merely the remains of a crashed weather balloon. Until well into the 1970s, the public and the vast majority of the media were satisfied with this explanation—until suddenly new rumors emerged from military circles, of all places. It was the birth of the biggest UFO conspiracy theory of all time. In December 2005, Walter Haut died—the press officer who had astonished the world public of his time. Could he and his hastily issued 1947 press release perhaps have been right? He did not

want to take the secret with him to the grave and shortly before his death, left behind a notarized, sworn statement, which clearly indicates that the salvaged wreckage had in fact been the remains of an extraterrestrial spaceship, including corpses of the crew, and the weather balloon story was only promoted to distract from the actual events.

According Haut's statement, which was made available to the public for the first time in 2007 in the book *Witness to Roswell*, by Thomas Carey and Donald Schmitt, the objects were reportedly recovered and brought to so-called "Building

84" on the Air Force base at Roswell. Haut claimed further in his statement that he and the then commanding officer and later Major Gen. William H. Blanchard themselves saw the 16 x 6 ½ feet (5 x 2 meter) oval object and the dead crew members. Haut also confirmed that there had been another crash in Corona, a few miles away. According to Haut's statement, the wreck had no windows at all and was without wings or landing gear. Haut described the crew as about four feet (1.2 meters) tall with disproportionately large heads. In his own words: "I am convinced that I saw a vehicle and its crew from outer space." Skeptics would now argue that Haut's statement is merely another big scam and that the conspiracy theorists were again trying their best. But the matter is not that simple. Walter Haut's declaration is in accordance, in very decisive points, with the details given by former CIA agent Chase Brandon, who on June 23, 2012, that is, sixty-five years after the incident, confirmed in a radio interview that the photos he saw with his own eyes in the CIA archives in the 1990s, definitely were not of a balloon, but rather, with ninety-nine percent probability, the ominous wreckage was that of remains of a UFO. Brandon on the radio show *Coast to Coast AM* said: "It was an aircraft that clearly did not come from this planet; it crashed, and I don't doubt one second that the words 'remains' and 'cadavers' state exactly what people were talking about. For me, this was definitely a pivotal moment, which confirmed that everything I believed in and I knew of, that so many other people believed, had actually happened. It was no weather balloon—it was what people had first reported."

Virtually nothing was published in German-language newspapers about the former CIA agent's explosive revelations; only the British tabloid *Daily Mail* reported Brandon's revelations in its July 9, 2012, issue, on the sixty-fifth anniversary of the Roswell crash. Was this report

Image of a supposedly surviving crew member of the alleged UFO that reportedly crashed in Roswell.

only considered a hoax in Germany and many other countries, or was there an ultimate intention behind this? The Roswell case is like all myths where there is a rumored conspiracy theory in its history: The more people join in, the less credible and more abstruse the matter becomes. But should we totally ignore either Walter Haut's affidavit or the revelations of former CIA agent Brandon, who after all, worked undercover for the US intelligence agency for twenty-five years? UFO advocates, in any case, feel that their stance on the existence of extraterrestrial life today was confirmed. They never doubted for a second that a spaceship and its entire crew actually came down in the desert of New Mexico in June 1947. At least in the case of Walter Haut's statement, it should be noted that he did not allow the publication of his statement until after his death. Thus, there can be no talk of a publicity stunt.

And with respect to the statements of ex-CIA man Brandon, nuclear physicist and Ufologist

Truth or legend? It is all the same for most visitors to Roswell. The small town is basically living on the myth of UFO crash and even has its own UFO museum. (Dykstra)

Nuclear physicist and ufologist Stanton T. Friedman suspected that the weather balloon theory was a diversionary tactic and did not correspond to the facts. (Allen)

Stanton T. Friedman is in no way surprised about his revelations. Friedman had never been satisfied with the US Army's explanation. For him, it was clear from the outset that the weather balloon theory was nothing but a pure scam. Why should the Army have an interest in sealing off the entire area around the crash site due to a simple weather balloon and also put pressure on members of the military and civilians from the region if they said anything on the incident? Friedman had visited the crash site already in the 1970s, to find out what really happened there. He spoke to eyewitnesses and finally formed his own picture of the events in Roswell. Among the witnesses was Major Jesse Marcel.

In 1947, Marcel was the chief of the rescue squad and virtually the first man on the spot, and he also confirmed to Friedman that what he and his people had found there in the desert could in no way have been a weather balloon

Business in UFO souvenirs is booming in Roswell—here mini-aliens complete with UFO. On the box is a map of the alleged crash site. (Schwede archive)

but that these parts had an extraterrestrial origin. For Friedman, it became clear from that moment that one of the greatest deceptions of all time had been launched in Roswell—he, therefore, recently stated in an interview with an Internet news service: "It is time that the mystical part of this story, of which we have long not put all the pieces together, is retired and replaced by the true story of what really happened."

If there is something to the theory of extraterrestrial visitors, then one of the interesting questions would certainly be: What would lead a UFO to land on Earth? The Russian UFO researcher Alexander Semenov believes he knows the reason—or one of them. According to Semenova's information, the many nuclear tests conducted at that time in the New Mexico desert were responsible. These tests caused a tremendous output of energy, which in turn was probably noticed by the crew of the wrecked ship and caused them to look into what was going on. But Roswell is certainly not the only unresolved UFO puzzle. Some thirty-three years later, there was another incident involving a supposedly alien spacecraft—this time in Europe.

7. The Rendlesham Incident

Woodbridge is a small port town right on the British North Sea coast and was a center for boat building, rope making, and sail making in the Middle Ages. In fact, King Edward III and Sir Francis Drake once had their warship fleets built in Woodbridge. Many tourists from home and abroad visit Woodbridge, especially in the summer months, to, in typical British style, find peace and quiet in the small, dignified coastal town. The peace and seclusion of Woodbridge was also held in high regard by the US Armed Forces, albeit rather for strategic reasons. No wonder that Americans selected the approximately nine-square-mile (fifteen sq km) forest area, primarily made up of pine plantations, heath, and moorlands, as a suitable location for their air force base. But the night of December 26–27, 1980, put an abrupt end to the tranquility: The base received an unusual visit. The incident quickly became a matter of discussion, which was not surprising, since Europe was dominated by the Cold War; there were atomic weapons stored at the air force complex and every little incident meant high alert for the security forces.

What happened? December 26, 1980: Senior security officer James Penniston was busy writing the rosters for the coming week, when suddenly a sergeant rushed into his office and excitedly reported an unusual light phenomenon directly over the pine forest. Penniston first calmed the man and thought it was nothing extraordinary. What could be going on, Penniston thought and buried himself again in his work. Guards had frequently seen strange lights, but most afterward turned out to be harmless. But then he thought of the nuclear weapons that were stored on the premises and the site commander's order to look into any unusual sighting—so Penniston informed the deputy commander, Lieutenant Colonel Charles Halt. The latter immediately

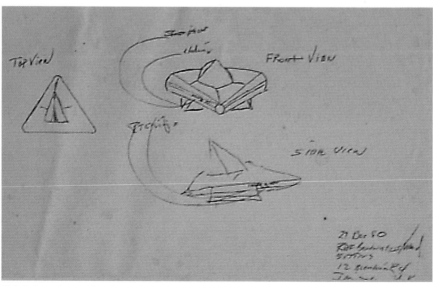

This is how James Penniston sketched the UFO said to have landed on the Air Force base at Woodbridge the night of December 26, 1980.

The glade in Rendlesham Forest where the UFO was sighted, according to eyewitnesses.

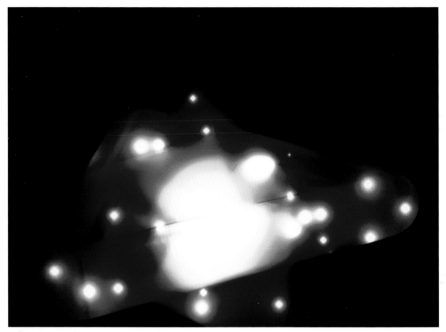

The triangular, pyramidal UFO of Rendlesham Forest would have looked like this.

assembled a security team, which also included Edward Cabansag and John Burroughs. Led by James Penniston, the men finally were on their way to make sure all was well, equipped with lamps, measuring devices, and tape recorders. The road led directly into the densely wooded pine plantation of Rendlesham Forest. After approximately 900 yards or more (a few hundred meters), the squad saw something that resembled a laser beam, which was directed towards the arsenal where the nuclear weapons were stored. Penniston, Cabansag, and Burroughs pulled back alarmed, taking cover and first thinking of an ambush attack. But who were the attackers—and especially, what did they want?

For many years, speculation prevailed about the further events in Woodbridge—and soon UFO researchers and esoteric scientists around the world were drawing close parallels to Roswell. Except that no UFO crashed here; instead it had apparently landed. There was some kind of contact between Penniston and his men and the crew. Soon the facts were changing as fast as they had in the case of Roswell—new findings were continually being added, were just as soon rebutted and finally assessed as fraud or hallucinations. Only twenty-seven years later, on November 12, 2007, at the press conference at the National Press Club in Washington, DC, did James Penniston describe the dramatic minutes in detail:

There was a bright light that radiated from an object on the forest floor. When we arrived there on foot, we could see the outline of a triangular aircraft of about nine feet long and six feet high. The aircraft was completely intact and was in a small clearing in the forest. As we approached, we had problems with our radio contact. That's why I asked Cabansag to stay behind, to relay radio messages to headquarters and thus to act as a relay. I went to the aircraft together with Burroughs. When we came up to the triangular aircraft, there were blue and yellow lights, swirling around the surface exterior, as if they were part of it. The air around us was electrically charged. We could feel it in our clothes, skin, and hair. Nothing in my training had prepared me for such a situation. After ten minutes with no sign of aggression, I decided that the aircraft was probably not hostile either to my team or the base. According to safety regulations, we conducted a full investigation on site; these included a complete physical examination of the aircraft, taking photos, and making notebook entries, which I did at that time, and radio announcements to headquarters. That was compulsory. On one side of the craft, there were symbols that were three inches high and two-and-a-half feet wide. These symbols were pictorial.

The largest of these was a triangle, which was in the middle between the others. These symbols were etched into the surface of the aircraft, which felt warm, and although it looked like black onyx, it felt like metal. During this investigation, I knew that I had never seen any such aircraft before. I haven't found it in the manual of known aircraft or anywhere else. After about forty-five

Another illustration of the UFO of Rendlesham Forest. Is it perhaps the same object reportedly spotted several times over Belgium almost nine years later?

minutes, the aircraft light began to get stronger. My men and I went on the defensive and got away from the aircraft, as it lifted off the ground with no noise or air vortex. It maneuvered through the trees and darted out of them with incredible speed. It was gone in the blink of an eye. In my notebook I noted: Velocity: IMPOSSIBLE. That night, more than eighty Air Force staff, all trained observers of the 81st Security Forces Squadron, were able to see the launch. The results of the investigation were forwarded through military channels. The team and witnesses were ordered to treat the investigation as Top Secret, and further discussions about it were banned.

On the two following days as well, mysterious lights were seen repeatedly in the area of Rendlesham Forest, but the base security personnel could not find any natural explanation for them. On the night of December 28–29, an object about thirty-three feet (ten meters) in diameter and shaped like a flat disk, appeared in the forest. It was reported that the object was wrapped in a yellowish mist that caused a lot of technical equipment to malfunction, and that the security staff at the site could feel a high-voltage electric field. The object is said to have remained on the ground for more than five hours and have then split into three objects that flew away in different directions. What witnesses experienced in the nights in question on site, officials are still keeping secret from the public; instead, it was later claimed to the press that the witnesses had only seen a missile re-entry into the Earth's atmosphere, or the light of a nearby lighthouse—statements that have obviously never satisfied experts. They wanted to know more and would not let go in their efforts to get on the track of the truth. As a result, many books have appeared over the years on the

incidents in Rendlesham Forest, which deal extensively with the eyewitnesses and objects seen on the nights in question. Always new, sometimes controversial details have been made public. Journalist and former detective Georgina Bruni has dealt extensively with the case and, in 2000, published a book titled *You Can't Tell the People*, in which witnesses and those responsible have their say. When Georgina Bruni had listened to all the witnesses and the book was ready to print, she learned from Charles Halt that he still had four to five hours of tape recordings in his desk drawer, which they could not possibly publish. According to Halt's information, there had been further incidents during the night in question, which were not recorded in the log. At first, Georgina Bruni had little use for all this, but she noted that there was more behind this case and that the Rendlesham Forest incident could possibly be the greatest event in human history. Charles Halt explained that the public is not yet ready to take cognizance of all the facts about the Rendlesham incident and concluded by saying: "What happened there is so extraordinary that publication of the exact events would put into question the whole way we humans see reality and the nature of the universe."

This is why Georgina Bruni decided to give her book the title *You Can't Tell the People*. Gradually, more and more eyewitnesses have broken their silence. These even included James Penniston, who had also touched the object. In 1994, he was questioned under hypnosis about the events and finally put under massive pressure by the US intelligence agency AFOSI (Office of Special Investigation Air Force), which coordinated Air Force activities outside of the United States jointly with the CIA. Among other things, the agents treated Penniston with a truth drug, to get to all the facts and, in addition, weaken his memory. Under hypnosis, Penniston reportedly stated that he had also made contact with the occupants of the object, and this statement was

The US Air Force comments to the press were to the effect that the witnesses had only observed the re-entry of a missile into the Earth's atmosphere or the light of a nearby lighthouse. (Merret)

also confirmed by the other witnesses who were on the spot with Penniston. Speaking on US television in 1994, Penniston said there were human occupants in the landed craft, who reportedly told him that they came from a future time on Earth, which they had laid waste, and this made any more normal reproduction impossible. Therefore, they came to get healthy "seed material." In 2009, finally, the British tabloid *The Sun* claimed that, suddenly and literally overnight, it could finally explain the Rendlesham Forest events. They had tracked down a now-retired sixty-six-year-old engineer named Peter Turtill from Ipswich, who was supposed to be responsible for all the spookery in the area. As *The Sun* reported, Turtill was driving a borrowed truck in the area at the relevant time. The vehicle broke down in Rendlesham Forest and Turtill reportedly found stolen fertilizer on the truck. Turtill was afraid he would get into trouble with the police; in trying to eliminate all his tracks, he set the vehicle on fire, which caused a series

of explosions and the truck burned brightly for several hours. Why Turtill had waited twenty-nine years to give his version of events, however, the tabloid could not explain. This one question has since been posed by many UFO researchers who have dealt with the incidents in Rendlesham Forest.

In any case, it is again the small details in the witness statements that make a serious assessment of what happened so difficult. Not without reason, the incident is, therefore, now regarded by many UFO researchers as the "European Roswell." Here again, the facts have only been released to the public piecemeal over the course of time, so that in the end, no one knows what is fact and what invention. One possible logical explanation among many would be that a secret test aircraft or a type of drone landed in Rendlesham Forest during the nights in question—possibly similar to the object that also made a stir in Belgium ten years later. More on this in the next chapter.

8. The Secret of the Black Triangles

At first it was just a small, marginal report; hardly anyone took any notice of it and it was soon forgotten. "Mysterious black triangles in the Belgian province of Liege," ran the headlines of Belgian daily newspapers on November 9, 1989. What supposedly happened was that a few oddballs had once again let themselves have a joke and wanted to make a public splash. But the triangle sightings would continue and soon cause a stir all over Belgium and the rest of the world. The story started out in the small town of Esneux in the province of Liège, on November 7, 1989. A police officer, who asked not to be named, recalls:

It was a warm day in late autumn, the sun had already set, and you could see a magnificent starry sky. I was on duty at the border station on the E40 international highway at Lichtenbusch. Since, as usual, there wasn't much going on that day, I had lots of time to look out the window. So, it must have been around 5:00 p.m., when a low-flying object with two or three glaring headlights caught my attention. It was flying at low altitude, just under a half-mile (500 meters) away over the border."

View over the tranquil town of Esneux in Liège province. It was here that one of the black triangles reportedly appeared for the first time on November 7, 1989, followed by a veritable wave of sightings. (Grandmont)

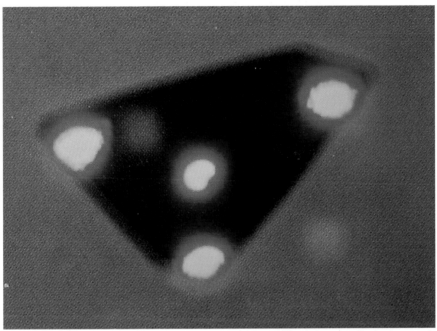

This photo went around the world at the beginning of the 1990s and reportedly shows one of the triangles sighted over Belgium. Since then, experts have been arguing whether the image is a forgery or not. (SOBEPS)

The police officer first thought of a helicopter. But it was flying too disproportionately low for that, and also was completely silent. The object followed the E40 towards Eupen. The policeman was not to be the last witness who would observe the object that night. For two policemen, Hubert Montigny and Heinrich Nicoll, the evening of November 7 is fixed in their memories. The two officers were on patrol on the N68 road, traveling towards Eynatten, when Montigny's interest was aroused by a bright spot to the right of the road. Something here seemed strange to the police: "It was as bright as the floodlights in football stadium." But Montigny immediately realized that it could not be floodlighting, because there was nothing except green pasture land in the entire area and certainly no football stadium.

The source of the light must, therefore, be something else. Meanwhile, the floodlights seemed to be steering closer towards the two police officers' vehicle. As the unknown light source hovered over the two officers, at just about 400 feet (120 meters) in the air and about 164 feet (fifty meters) from the road, it was so bright, according to their statement, that you could have read a newspaper by it. Montigny immediately wound down the window on his side of the car to see the unusual light at close range. The policeman turned his gaze upward, but the light was so bright that he had to protect his eyes with his right hand. Looking between his fingers, Montigny saw that the light source came from a large, dark platform hovering motionless in the sky, which had three huge

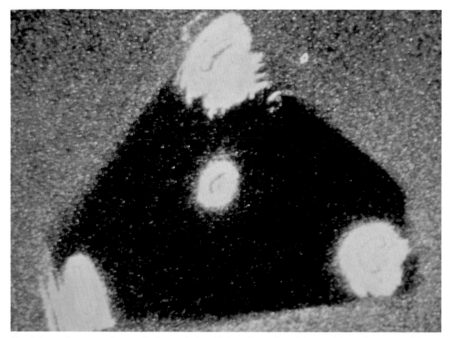

The false color computer analysis carried out later shows that this must have been a solid body. This was reportedly where the rotation of the three lights could be seen. (SOBEPS)

spotlights on its underside. The two policemen described the thing to journalists later as a completely silent, isosceles triangle with a broad base, attached corners that looked like they were cut into, and with a red light rotating at the center. Montigny described the object's dimensions as about 82 x 98–114 feet (25 x 30-35 meters) with a height of approximately 6 1/2 feet (2 meters). Montigny first assumed it was a new type of American test aircraft and asked for the nearest military airport. At first, they knew of nothing, but confirmed that they too had a signal on their radar that they could not explain.

The policemen pursued the object further, which continued its flight along the N68 to Eupen at a speed of around thirty-one mph (fifty km/h), and meanwhile had now been seen by other witnesses—who also couldn't find any explanation

for the object. Many of the witnesses were initially perturbed because the events simply were beyond anything they could imagine; others shouted in fear to the police. From then on, Montigny and Nicoll wouldn't let the object out of their sight. Meanwhile, the triangle remained stationary above the Gileppe dam. The platform moved almost silently. Only a light humming noise, like that from an electric motor, was heard, as the two policemen later reported to journalists: "It was now 2 1/2 miles (four km) away, but it was clearly visible." What followed left the eyewitnesses present breathless: The next moment, "rays" emerged from the object, consisting of two thin, reddish light beams, that shot rapidly out of the object with a red ball at their ends. Shortly afterward, the two balls turned back to the triangle. The spectacle was repeated several times. The police estimated the rays later at between about .5–1 miles (1–2 km) long.

At about 6:45 p.m., another such triangle appeared, but soon again retreated into the night sky at a phenomenal speed. The first object still remained for a while over the dam. The two policemen had the opportunity to examine the object for a long time and realized that there was an internally illuminated dome with rectangular windows on the platform. The eerie spectacle reportedly ended only after two hours. Due to the extensive coverage in the local press in the following days, 140 more witnesses claimed that they had also observed the triangle. In the next few days as well, the wave of sightings continued in Belgium. Sightings were reported from across the country almost daily. And these objects were almost always one or more "black triangles." Belgian military fighter interceptors were then sent out for reconnaissance—but returned without tangible results. Belgium was puzzled. The Belgian Defense Minister Guy Come himself stated his position to the international press on the events and concluded that: "Any possibility that this might have been a military plane has been thoroughly reviewed by us and was definitely excluded." Soon after, a request was sent to the Pentagon in Washington, DC, and according to an internal situation report by the DIA , the news service of the US Defense Department, it was said later on: "... The US Air Force confirmed to the Belgian Air Force and the Belgian Ministry of Defense that no US Air Force stealth bomber was operating at the relevant time period in the Ardennes." The speculation was endless, and the story of the black triangles eventually even made it onto the RTL (Radio Television Luxembourg) program *Explosive* on February 25, 1990. There, German UFO skeptic Rudolf Henke presented the hypothesis that the mysterious aircraft were in all likelihood only one or more ultra-light aircraft. The Belgian

military soon turned to the UFO organization SOBEPS (Société Belge d'étude of Phénomènes Spatiaux) with a request for assistance in the investigation of these mysterious events, because the wave of sightings in Belgium continued into the following year as well. On the night of March 30–31, 1990, strange objects reappeared on the radar screen at the Beauvechain Air Force base. In addition, on the night in question there were at least a dozen reports by police officers and civilians to the local police stations, again on the subject of mysterious triangles. Around midnight, two NATO F-16 fighter interceptors finally took off to track down the mysterious aircraft. According to the Belgian Air Force General Staff official report, in three cases the pilots were even able to make visual contact with the flying craft. At about 12:13 a.m., the first UFO was sighted at a distance of a little more than six miles (ten km) directly in front of the fighters, at 9,000 feet in the air. Its speed was around 172 mph (278 km/h). At that moment, when the fighter aircraft's target radar turned on, the object accelerated within seconds to more than 1,118 mph (1,800 km/h), escaped the F-16—while at the same time it descended to 5,000 feet, to then immediately ascend again to 11,000 feet. Shortly afterward, it descended close to the ground. At around 12:30 a.m., the UFO was re-tracked to 5,000 feet altitude—this time at 851 mph (1,370 km/h); the automatic target tracking was activated again and again radar contact was lost. At 1:00 a.m., the object finally disappeared without a trace. There has been no explanation for this flight maneuver up until today. According to air force reports, it is at least the case that no conventional aircraft can perform such rapidly changing flight maneuvers. The report stated literally: "... the measured velocities and the observed alterations in altitude exclude the hypothesis that this could involve any confusion with airplanes. In addition, the slow movements displayed in other phases are not typical of aircraft. Despite repeatedly breaking through the sound barrier, no shock wave was ever felt nor was any boom heard. There is no explanation for this." Several witnesses, including five police officers, also observed the fighter's pursuit of the UFO from the ground. At about 12:30 a.m., officers from the highway patrol on N29, in the direction of Namur, saw a "flickering light" and two aircraft that pursued it. And they saw that the light constantly tried to avoid the jet fighters. At about 2:00 a.m., eyewitness Marcel Alfarano filmed an object over Brussels, which had a large round searchlight on each of its three corners and a fourth pulsing red light in the middle. In its 700-page report, titled "Wave of UFOs over Belgium," SOBEPS came to the conclusion: "... that lately there have been a large number of anomalous phenomena in Belgian airspace, for which there is no natural explanation; however, investigations also found that at no time could any aggressive behavior by the invaders be established, which in turn suggests the conclusion that the visitors currently constitute no immediate threat. We analyzed more than 2,000 reports of sightings, plus half a dozen photos and films—they all apparently leave no doubt that the objects over Belgium are not of terrestrial origin."

In a 2011 RTL report, it was presumed, however, that photos of the triangles are skillful scams: What is probably the best photo of the triangles, which went around the world and was shot by a certain P.M. in April 1990, using a Practika camera, is a forgery, according to RTL research. A shock to science, since after all, international scientists had been working on precisely this photo for more than two decades.

The image, which until now at least had been the best proof of the triangles' existence, was thoroughly investigated from various viewpoints and found to be genuine. In July 2011, according

to RTL information, a certain Patrick was said to have confessed that he, together with a colleague, cut the triangle out of a 31.5 inch (eighty cm) wide block of Styrofoam, and then hung it from the ceiling and photographed it. He remorsefully admitted on camera, when asked the reason for his belated confession, that after all, he had fooled the world with this photo—now he finally wanted to put an end to the spookery. In great detail, he told the RTL reporter how he had cut the triangle to the shape and that he only used commercially available flashlights as lighting, that he had fastened the block to a fishing line, and finally hung it up—then simply pressed the button, and thus, what was probably the most successful and, up to today, the most authentic photo of one of the black triangles probably ever photographed, was taken. Did the author fool all of science for more than two decades this way? Renowned scientists, however, appeared surprised when all this was published after more than twenty years. They included physicist August Meesen from the Catholic University of Leuven, who had repeatedly examined the photo and found many interesting anomalies in it, which could not be so easily explained by a forgery— it would be impossible, according to Meesen, that the lights on the photo came from a normal flashlight, because no standard hand flashlight could be the source of such an intense and strong light. Meesen visited the alleged counterfeiter, accompanied by an RTL reporter team, and asked him specific questions on how the photo was produced, and Meesen mostly got only one response: "I don't know." Meesen also did a color analysis of the photo, which produced the amazing result, that while the triangle can be seen on the blue layer, it cannot be on the red. A process that Meesen cannot explain. In conclusion, again in this case, there are more questions than answers. According to information from UFO researcher Renaud Leclet, at least

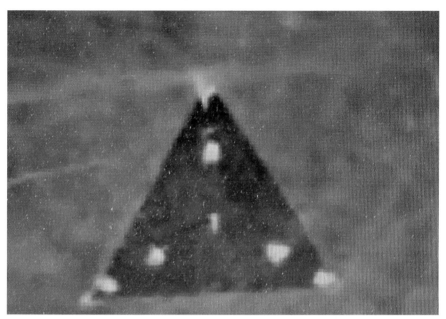

In the past, huge triangles were supposedly sighted all over the world, of which there are also numerous photos. But the issue of whether they are faked or real still hasn't been settled. Here, an image of a UFO over Australia, allegedly taken from Google Earth.

some of the nocturnal sightings could be explained by the deployment of military helicopters, and Central Exploration Network for Extraordinary Celestial Phenomena (CENAP), under Werner Walter, also came to this view; they merely attribute the rapid change of position on the existing radar images to radar interference due to meteorological effects. Other UFO skeptics see the wave of sightings in Belgium as another self-reinforcing psychological process, that was triggered by the numerous media reports and encouraged others to report their own misinterpreted observations.

Belgium, however, would not remain an isolated case. At the beginning of the 1990s, sightings of black triangles appeared across Europe, even in distant Russia. The high commander of the Soviet Air Force, Colonel General Igor Maltsev, confirmed a case in an official statement; this occurred at 9:00 p.m. in Zagorsk, around twenty-

nine miles (forty-seven km) northeast of Moscow on March 21, 1990. Just five minutes after the first appearance of an unidentified flying object in the airspace over Zagorsk, the crew of a MiG-29 was ordered to start pursuing the object. The official incident report stated: Unidentified flying object at 6,000 feet in the air. For almost one hour, the MiG criss-crossed the alleged area of operation without finding a trace. The pilots were unable to see anything, either on their radar, or in the sky. Not until around 10:00 p.m. did the crew of the fighter see two strange flashing lights in the night sky, and soon they were able to recognize the shadowy outline of the object. According to the pilot, this case also involved a triangular flying craft. Via radio, the crew requested the uninvited intruder to land immediately. But what followed astounded the MiG crew: On their on-board radar, the experienced pilots watched the triangle, about 12.5 miles (twenty km) away, begin to regularly "jump" across a distance of about sixty-two miles (100 km) in less than a minute. From the data, they calculated that the object must have reached a speed of 3,728 mph (6,000 km/h). Such an airspeed and the corresponding maneuvers are currently impossible with conventional aircraft. There was little chance for the crew of the MiG to catch the uninvited guest, but the pilots did not give up so quickly. During the following minutes, they tried again and again to approach nearer to the sinister object—but the intruder, using its inexplicable maneuvers, always kept a step ahead of the pursuers. Soon after, however, the pilots, flying in a steep curve, succeeded in getting closer to the object until it was just under 1,500 feet away from them.

Now for the first time, the MiG crew could see more details of the flying craft. According to the pilots, the object was "a triangle with two flashing lights." The pilots did not dare approach the object any nearer, since they did not know what the flying craft was still capable of and whether this fact meant they were facing a security incident. It also seemed to the Soviet side that they would now be confronted with the fact that there was probably an intelligence involved that was technically years ahead of us. Colonel General Igor Maltsev literally stated that: "We have good reasons to declare that the UFOs were in no way visual hallucinations or a global psychosis. They were located on radar; pictures are analyzed by experts."

Russia's military leadership reacted anxiously to the reports of the sinister invaders, confirming indirectly that it "must involve a very advanced intelligence that intervened in our airspace and, in effect, exposed our technology." In an interview with the magazine *Literary Gazeta*, General Ivan Tretyak went even one step further and advised the military against any attacks on the objects

". . . should it turn out that at least some UFOs are the product of a highly organized intelligence of a much more developed civilization than ours, every struggle against these objects and their crews could—before we are sure about their intentions—have devastating consequences."

Just what the "visitors" were capable of, the crew of the radar station in Kuybyshev in Tartary would learn on September 13, 1990. Shortly after midnight, a huge flying object appeared on the radar screen there. The strength of the radar echo was roughly comparable to that of a strategic bomber. The distance from the station was about sixty-two miles (one hundred km). The crew was ordered to check the radar echo more closely, which they did immediately. But already during the check, to the great astonishment of the radar operators, the echo disintegrated and turned into the size of a flock of birds. At the same moment, the huge object reappeared on the radar screen. This time, only about twenty-five miles (forty km) from the station. Immediately, several employees vacated the station to go to the underground bunker to check that everything was in order. They reported that what they saw amazed them. One of the station staff recalled: "We could see it clearly. It flew at [about] four miles (ten meters) in the air and had the shape of an isosceles triangle with rounded corners. The underside of the object was smooth, but not as smooth as glass—it looked like a layer of soot. It had neither openings nor hatches or landing devices. Everything we saw were white-blue light beams." Soon after, the object started to land close to the radar station. The staff member heard a rustling sound, as if a light gust of wind was blowing through leaves. The eyewitness described further that suddenly a flash shot sideways from a visible opening in the base, which was about three meters thick, that hit the radar antenna and caused it to collapse. Shortly thereafter, the steel frame was ablaze and the triangle launched itself again in just under an hour. After a thorough inspection, members of the military determined that all the steel parts had melted, except for the aluminum mirror. The staff later wondered about how much power would be needed to make steel burn, but they found no plausible answers.

One possible explanation might lie far away out in the desert of Nevada. This is where Area 51 lies—America's testing ground for super-secret aviation and aerospace research projects.

9. Area 51—America's Secret World

Sand and stones as far as the eye can see. I am located approximately eighty miles (130 km) northwest of the glittery world of Las Vegas on highway SR 375—the only road that leads to Groom Lake. This place is like the back of beyond. Far and wide, there's not a soul; the sky is steel blue; in the distance, the exteriors of half-abandoned villages, houses, and trailers are peeling away in the shimmering midday heat. The only inhabited place, which bears the name Rachel, is enthroned like a Biblical apparition on the horizon. Barely one hundred people live in this desert hell hole, only thirteen miles (twenty-one km) from the boundary of a restricted military zone, the former nuclear test site Yuka Flats, which is the size of Bavaria.

Since the late 1980s, Rachel has become the "UFO Capital of the World," as the locals tell me, a kind of place of pilgrimage for UFO enthusiasts from around the world, which is why the people here call Route 375 "Alien Highway."

Dalton, who has lived in the small town right on the border of Dreamland, for more than thirty years, points to the mighty Tikaboo Mountains and says grinning: "I've seen a lot of unusual things in the sky and I'm sure they all come from the base over there." The Little A'Le'Inn (pronounced "Little Alien," a kind of pun) is the last place to stop before the base. It is a saloon, bar, and motel in one and offers, besides a few rooms, a whole bunch of UFO photos on the walls and all sorts of odds and ends that make the hearts

Groom Lake Road leads directly into "Dreamland," which has meanwhile become the byword for conspiracy theorists around the world for secret UFO research.

The locals call Route 357 the "Extraterrestrial Highway."

of UFO enthusiasts beat faster. Anyone who has the courage to drive up to the gates of the Area, now must finally leave the highway and take Groom Lake Road. It leads directly into "Dreamland," which has become the byword for conspiracy theorists around the world for secret UFO research. Area 51 is officially part of the 1.5 million hectare Nellis Air Force base (NAFB). The name Area 51 comes from the old area divisions on the maps of the Nevada test site. Wild stories circulate especially about the military base airport. Perhaps not entirely without reason. Civilian aircraft are strictly forbidden to fly over it, under threat of being fired at. Even Air Force pilots, if they are not authorized, have to give it a wide berth when they want to fly from A to B. So what's going on that is so mysterious? An old lady, who grew up in Rachel, waves it off, laughs loudly, and finally declares: "This is all hocus-pocus, nothing more. But tourism is booming, since everyone is talking about the Area and people come here from around the world. That's good, because who otherwise would wander into this deserted place?"

The sixty-two-mile-square- (100 square kilometer) sized Area 51 lies northeast of Groom Lake, a dry salt lake. After the Second World War, an Air Force base was established on the southern edge of the lake—surrounded by huge hangars, giant utility installations, radar facilities, and the longest runway in the world: the runway is 5.9 miles (9.6 km) long. It stretches from one shore of the lake to the other. There is a second takeoff and landing strip parallel to it. Conspiracy theorists suspect that most of the structures are located underground. The witness reports to this effect, but also official documents, which indicate that the geology of the region is particularly suitable for underground installations, supporting this theory. High fences and motion detectors along the edges of the Area protect it against unwanted visitors. Guards in white Jeeps patrol here

Since the late 1980s, Rachel had become the "UFO Capital of the World," as the locals say, a kind of place of pilgrimage for UFO enthusiasts from around the world.

constantly and energetically rebuke every curious visitor—if necessary by threatening further measures. Motion detectors and video cameras are hidden everywhere in the desert terrain. Crossing the boundary is punishable with a $5,000 fine and a year in prison, as is written in large letters on the sign. That's everyday life there, people from Rachel tell me. They have become used to it. There is probably no other place in the United States that is as closely guarded as this small desert hell hole. Until April 1995, you could still see the base from the summit of the approximate one-mile-(1,800 meter) high White Sands mountain and the neighboring Freedom Ridge mountain saddle, but then these two viewpoints were commandeered by the military and closed to visitors. Now you can only get a look at the base from the summit of one and one-half mile (2,500 meter) high Tikaboo Peak, some twenty-six miles (forty-two km) away. The view is bad on unfavorable days

when a haze spreads over the region, but on a clear day, you can still just make out a part of the installations with the naked eye, even from this distance.

Originally, Groom Lake was used during the Second World War as a bomb and artillery firing range. Then the site was shut down until 1955, when representatives of the top-secret "Skunk Works" discovered the site as a suitable place for test flights of its Lockheed U-2 spy plane. In the engineers' view, the lake offered ideal takeoff and landing conditions, and the Tikaboo Valley protected it from the prying eyes of the public. In August 1955, the first U-2 took off here on its maiden flight, and a year later, the CIA launched their spy flights over the Soviet Union from that base. Even before completion of development work on the U-2, Lockheed started work on its successor project "A-12 Oxcart" at Groom Lake—a reconnaissance aircraft that was supposed to fly at 1,864 mph (3,000 km/hour). Not only the

Many secret projects were developed in Area 51 in the course of history. These also included the high-tech Northrop B-2 Spirit stealth bomber. (USAF)

The Mach 3 fast Lockheed A-12 was also developed and tested in Area 51. (CIA)

A-12's flight characteristics, but also its enormous maintenance requirements made extensive expansion of the test facility necessary at Groom Lake. Right in time for the first flight of the A-12, in 1962, the main runway was extended to 1.6 miles (2,600 meters) and the base was now manned by a fixed personnel of around 1,000 men. It also had its own fuel depot, and a tower with the call sign "Dreamland" was constructed, which later became a symbol of the whole

View of Groom Lake and Papoose Lake. (Searls)

installation. From this time, the region around Area 51 was declared a high security zone. Anyone who entered the premises illegally could be immediately shot without warning.

Many secret prototypes were developed at Area 51 in the course of history, including such prominent models as the Lockheed F-117 Nighthawk and the Northrop B-2 Spirit stealth bomber. But these are only the official projects. According to unconfirmed information from former staff, reportedly much more was developed and built there over the past five decades— projects of which the public has never heard anything about. In the past, press reports repeatedly provided grist for the rumor mill on Area 51. In 1988, the *New York Times* reported about a top-secret stealth aircraft, which would be developed at Groom Lake. Was this the B-2 bomber or perhaps an aircraft whose existence remains unknown to this day?

The military journal *Gung Ho* reported many years ago in one of its issues about a technology that is beyond all imagination. James C. Goudall, author of the said article and an expert on radar technology, wrote:"We have things flying around there in the Nevada desert that would stagger the imagination of George Lucas. Many of the machines developed there apparently have a technology that leaves conventional aircraft far behind." This statement can also be confirmed by former US Air Force employee Edgar Rothschild Fouche. Rothschild Fouche was, as one would say in army circles, an insider who has knowledge about many operations in Area 51. In his book *Alien Rapture*, published in 1998, Rothschild Fouche confirms that the US government's so-called "Black Budget" operates projects, none of which are known to the public. Rothschild Fouche is speaking here of a technology that is hard to imagine, even using the greatest possible imagination. Thus, it is the fine, small details on technology and weapons that could freeze the reader's blood, because these simply sound so absurd, yet still so frighteningly real and detailed, that they cannot possibly be invented. Although many chapters in his book give more the impression of a work of science fiction when you read them, and in the end, the author must even frankly admit that, because of his non-disclosure agreement with the government, he could only use the facts in a novel, yet much of what Rothschild Fouche describes, together with co-author Brad Steiger, may well be true. So it is not surprising that since the book was published, Edgar Rothschild Fouche's life has changed. He lives more dangerously, is constantly on the alert, and feels persecuted. He has claimed that he has received more than a dozen death threats in the past, his home and car have been broken into several times, and he has been denounced on the Internet as a liar and a forger. Again and again, therefore, Rothschild Fouche has raised the question of who really is behind all this and who has an interest in publicly damaging his reputation in this way?

In his book, Edgar Rothschild Fouche says that he is fully convinced that there is a long list of "Black Budget" projects and that, besides the known projects over the past four decades, a whole series of types have been launched of which the public has never heard, and that many people in numerous states and even abroad have seen these flying, especially during the night hours, but about which nothing has ever become public.

In the little town of Rachel, it is no secret that objects are constantly being sighted that have no association with any known type of aircraft. Strange lights that blaze their trail in crazy flight movements through the cold, starry desert nights,

Local residents, as well UFO pilgrims, constantly report that they see unusual flying objects over the base, such as this snapshot of a "flying saucer." The picture looks blurry and out of focus, which suggests that it was taken from many miles/kilometers distant with a powerful telephoto lens. Incidentally, this is always one of the problems with "evidence" of alleged UFO photos.

DEPARTMENT OF THE AIR FORCE
WASHINGTON DC 20330-1000

Office of the Secretary

AUG 1998

Dear

This responds to your letter to the Secretary of the Air Force regarding "Area 51."

Neither the Air Force nor the Department of Defense owns or operates any location known as "Area 51." There are a variety of activities, some of which are classified, throughout what is often called the Air Force's Nellis Range Complex. There is an operating location near Groom Dry Lake. Specific activities and operations conducted on the Nellis Range, both past and present, remain classified and cannot be discussed publicly.

We hope this information is helpful.

Sincerely

JEFFREY A. RAMMES, Major, USAF
Chief, White House Inquiry Branch
Office of Legislative Liaison

The written statement by the US Air Force about Area 51 on the Air Force base at Groom Lake.

eerie noises that sound like loud roars or rumbles chase through the mountains and echo far into the interior of Nevada and neighboring California. The people out here have become accustomed to all this, and above all: they believe in what Rothschild Fouche wrote in his book. They indeed do not know what goes on behind the gates of Area 51, but they know what they have seen with their own eyes. One proof that unusual things happen around Groom Lake is provided by a video taken by an American television network a few years ago. It showed many lights over the mountains of Groom Lake, which moved through the picture in serpentine tracks and finally remained completely quiet and stationary. No aircraft and helicopters with conventional technology would be capable of such maneuvers. The reliability of the video was confirmed, but no statement followed from the US government or military. Even the existence of Area 51 is not confirmed by official sources, only the Air Force base. Taken literally from a written US Air Force statement:

Area 51 is not an Air Force designation, but the area involved is part of Nellis AFB complex. This complex is used to test technologies and systems and to train for operations that are critical to the efficiency of the American Armed Forces and the security of the United States. Part of the complex is situated on dry Groom Lake. Some certain activities and operations that have been carried out at Nellis Range in the past and present, remain classified and cannot be discussed in public.

Edgar Rothschild Fouche knows that, in the past, there were many projects tested at Groom Lake that could be responsible for these strange flight activities around Area 51. In his view, one of the largest and most important projects in the history of US armaments is the "Aurora" project. For many years, there has been speculation about whether the name Aurora stands for a specific type of aircraft or for an entire project at the same time. According to Rothschild Fouche, it is well established that Aurora is a top secret air and space development program that was funded under the Strategic Defense Initiative (SDI) program by the National Reconnaissance Office, the National Security Agency, and the CIA. The SDI program included an entire package of extensive research and development projects—especially space-based weapons systems, which is why the public soon gave the project the

Still images from a video. The film reportedly shows the alleged TR-3B ASTRA over Paris. At the end of the film, it appeared in a white "plasma ring." Whether the video is real or a forgery, is not yet clear. (YouTube)

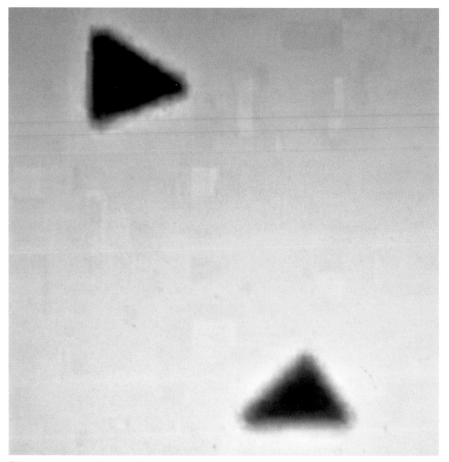

This picture comes from a video that allegedly was made during an exercise in Syria. It shows objects that are designated as the TR-3B and maneuver over the training grounds and temporarily remain stationary in one position.

nickname of the "Star Wars" program. Since 1988, the US government has invested an estimated $29 billion in the SDI program, but over time the government cut the funding back again, since it became known that the results were significantly below the high expectations. How many and, above all, which projects have been funded and expedited directly by means of the SDI, is still unclear, since most projects are classified as top secret. The existence of the

TR-3B ASTRA (Advanced Stealth Technology Recon Aircraft), is repeatedly mentioned in this connection; it is reportedly financed from SDI funds as part of the "Black Budget" projects. The TR-3B is reportedly an absolute high-tech aircraft, and no one could quite conceive of its technology, if they had not seen the thing with their own eyes, according to Rothschild Fouche. The author is even absolutely sure that the TR-3B was the aircraft involved in the en masse appearances over Europe and Russia, including in Belgium, at the beginning of the 1990s. Rothschild Fouche's information refers to data from a deceased former NSA agent, who is said to have confirmed the existence and operation of the TR-3B in all respects. However, the TR-3B did not have an anti-gravity system, as was at times speculated. Using a so-called scram-jet propulsion, the machine can reportedly achieve amazingly high speeds—in a range of more than Mach 9. A technology, therefore, that actually may still not be deployment-ready according to the official state of technology today, but apparently already exists in America's secret laboratories around Area 51.

The TR-3B, writes Rothschild Fouche in his book, is a high-tech reconnaissance and combat aircraft in one. The most modern weapon of war of all. The technology is reportedly stunning and unimaginable. Equipped with a so-called terahertz scanner, it is even possible to see through building walls. Terahertz scanner technology is essentially based on the function of "body scanners" which are meanwhile used in almost every major US airport—another technology that was developed and funded under "Black Budget" programs.

But who is able to produce such a revolutionary and ground-breaking technology as the TR-3B today? A possible clue leads in the Californian million-inhabitant city of San Diego, the eighth largest city in the United States. This is the headquarters of the Ryan Aeronautical Company, founded in 1934.

The company became famous due to, among other things, the legendary *Spirit of St. Louis*, in which Charles Lindbergh crossed the Atlantic in 1927. Later, the company focused more and more on construction of military technology, including in manufacturing unmanned reconnaissance aircraft and drones. The technology became ever-more complex over the years and few, if any, outsiders have even the slightest idea about

Real or forgery? An image that reportedly shows the TR-3B accompanied by a Boeing KC-135 tanker and two F-111s over the northern Trinity Bay of Galveston Bay.

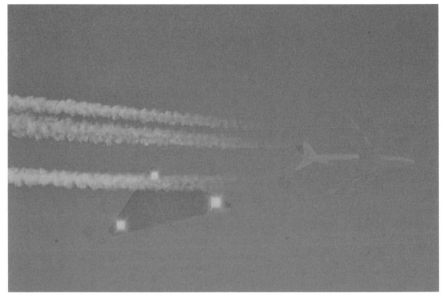

Another shot of the supposed TR-3B in daylight near a commercial airliner. It is unclear whether such images are genuine or doctored.

This image shows a TR-3B over the Grand Canyon. Again, the authenticity of the image has yet to be either proven or invalidated.

what is really going on behind the company doors. Many projects that originated here have been subject to the strictest secrecy, and this is still true today. Ryan Aeronautical's preferred customers include the US military and the intelligence services.

Engineer Robert W. Winters and colleague George R. Cota apparently succeeded in winning the really big coup in the mid-1970s. They developed, according to the present patent specification, a triangle with an extremely good flight performance, in the sense of air superiority, and which is almost one hundred percent invisible to the eye and radar. US patent 4019699A was issued on April 26, 1977, and contains a detailed technical drawing and the following description: "The aircraft has a very low observability both visually as well as on radar and acoustic tracking devices. The aircraft has few edges and surfaces, in the form of a delta wing, where the edges are straight or rounded at the crest. All surfaces are flat in terms of aerodynamic requirements; the entire surface of the aircraft is electrically conductive with minimal disruption. The propulsion system is shielded from radar by the wings." Winter and Cota's design resembles the description of the TR-3B in many aspects. Whether it actually is the TR-3B has yet to be proven. It is possible that this involves a previous version or a model that never went into serial production, but this, due to its striking resemblance to the sighted triangles, would be rather unlikely. Another possibility is that Lockheed Martin might produce the TR-3B. On August 2, 2011, two witnesses saw, on the premises of Lockheed Martin in Oswego in New York, a hovering triangle with three white lights at the corners and a red one in the middle. Then the object reportedly flew in the direction of Hickory Park. According to the witnesses, it was completely silent. It seems in any case to be an indisputable fact that something revolutionary was flying in the sky, which is the issue for numerous UFO sightings. Finally, a good half-dozen partially high-quality video recordings exist, which suggest that a secret aircraft has been in use for many years that the US government deliberately uses all means to keep secret. It is believed that the TR-3B is equipped with a so-called MHD (magnetohydrodynamic) generator, which is used to increase the output rate of exhaust gases in rocket engines to boost the engine performance level, among other things. The manned TR-3B does not have any windows, as per present information, and is flown by means of multiple cameras and a GPS system.

Experts also suspect that behind the supposed "beam weapons," there is a novel technology, still largely unknown to the public, which was also financed from SDI funds. This beam-emitter had multiple functions, according to the experts, including that it could also deliver microwave radiation. This technology should even make it possible to set markers and signs on the ground. Since 1994, reportedly at least three of these $9 billion wonder weapons have been deployed in the whole world, commissioned by the Tactical Reconnaissance Office, NASA, and the CIA, who, among others, also co-financed the project.

Evidence of this could be provided by observations of two eyewitnesses a few weeks before the European UFO wave in August 1989. The witnesses saw a huge "black triangle" over northern Trinity Bay in Galveston Bay clearly being fueled from a Boeing KC135. The duo was accompanied by two F-111 fighter aircraft. Witnesses repeatedly saw that the black triangles were escorted by army helicopters and fighter jets. A witness made such an observation from Houston in Texas on August 15, 2001. From his backyard, the witness saw a black triangle was

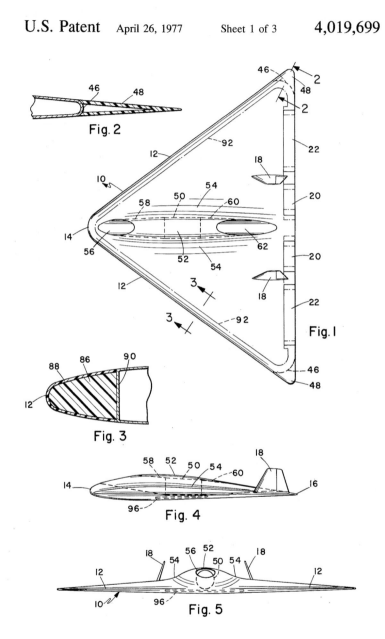

The drawing from the patent specifications of engineers Robert W. Winters and George R. Cota. In the mid-1970s, they designed an aircraft with supposedly superior flight characteristics intended to be almost invisible to the eye and radar.

Does this image support possible evidence of TR-3B?

flying silently at low altitude over a river. Then the object disappeared towards the NASA Johnson Space Center. Minutes later, a US Air Force F-16 jet appeared and accompanied the object. All this, of course, keeps raising the question in UFO research of whether or not this case ultimately involves totally earthly technology. Whether it is called the TR-3B or in the end bears a different name, probably plays a relatively minor role. It is assumed, in any event, that the US government has already been working for years on a technology that is ahead of the current official state-of-the-art by several decades, and that secret test bases are being used all over the entire United States, and that during past test flights of secret projects, even US citizens have repeatedly been harmed.

10. The Case of Betty Cash and Vickie Landrum

It was the evening of December 29, 1980, when fifty-one-year-old Betty Cash, together with her friend Vicki Landrum and her seven-year-old grandson, Colby, was driving home at about 9:00 p.m. from Houston to Dayton in Texas. During the evening, the three had tried in vain to find an open bingo hall; but because it was just before New Year's, all facilities in the area were closed. Betty Cash drove her car, an Oldsmobile Cutlass, homewards on Highway FM 1485, a farm-to-market road normally used only by locals, and at the time in question, there wasn't a vehicle in sight. Suddenly, Betty's attention was aroused, near the community of Huffman, by an unusual bright star that seemed to be moving. At first she thought it was an airplane landing at the twenty-two mile (thirty-five km) distant Houston Intercontinental Airport and had already lost sight of the strange light. But minutes later it was back, this time in the form of a brightly shining diamond. Now Vickie Landrum also saw the huge glowing object in the starry night sky. Since Vickie Landrum was deeply religious, she thought at first that the Biblical prophecy was now being fulfilled and calmed the frightened Colby in the back with the words: "That is Jesus, don't be afraid. He comes down from heaven and leads us people to a better place." But the seven-year-old wouldn't be calmed. Afraid, he crept ever further under the front seat and held

On the evening of December 29, 1980, fifty-one-year-old Betty Cash, her friend, Vickie Landrum, and her grandson, Colby, on their way from Houston to Dayton, saw a brightly shining diamond hovering over the highway.

Vickie Landrum and Betty Cash together in a family photo before the UFO sighting.

his hands protectively over his face. Vickie and Betty now also became frightened. The eerie UFO came down closer and soon was hovering at treetop height. Flames shot out of the bottom and struck the asphalt, which immediately began to melt. For safety, Betty steered towards the right shoulder of the road and stopped the car. The heat emanating from the diamond was almost unbearable and they could now also feel it inside the car. According to their further descriptions, the strange object seemed to lurch as if it was out of control. The three quickly got out of the car and stood on the road, where they could see the object better. Only now did they realize the real dimensions of the flying craft, which, in their words, was the size of a water tower, seemed to be made of some softly gleaming aluminum and was accompanied by a squadron of Army helicopters. The heat soon became unbearable

on the road as well, and the trio decided to continue watching from the air-conditioned car. In the car it was now so hot that even the vinyl dashboard was getting soft, and Betty left a clearly visible hand print when she touched it.

The fiery tail of the diamond was as bright as the light of a blowtorch, so that the witnesses had to cover their eyes for a while. After about four minutes, the object moved away again and the three were able to continue their trip. Yet they still saw the object with the helicopter squadron several times in the distance, before it disappeared entirely behind the trees of the nearby woods. The next morning, the three felt seriously ill. Vickie complained of an unbearable headache, Betty of severe nausea—her neck swelled up, and there were strange red spots all over her skin and face. All three also had typical symptoms of sunburn. Betty complained of constant nausea and diarrhea, her hair fell out in clumps, and after a few days, she became completely blind in one eye. Finally, she had to go to the hospital for several weeks, twice in succession, because her health deteriorated so rapidly. Vickie and Colby also suffered hair loss, developed ulcers, and lost their appetites. A radiologist later diagnosed radiation damage in all three eyewitnesses, which he said was caused by ionizing radiation in combination with infrared and UV light. This type of radiation source is usually found only in nuclear facilities or in military possession.

It does not occur in natural surroundings. Three years later, Betty Cash and Vickie Landrum became sick with cancer.

Yet journalist and UFO skeptic Philip J. Klass doubted the results of the examinations and claimed that the reports provided no reason for suspecting that the three witnesses had really been exposed to radiation in this concentration, and no increased radioactivity had been detected locally. Betty Cash died on December 29, 1999, at the age of seventy-one, eighteen years to the day after her encounter with the UFO. Vickie Landrum died on September 12, 2007, at the age of eighty-four. Ultimately it remained unclear whether their diseases resulted from increased levels of radiation.

The American UFO research group MUFON (Mutual UFO Network), which soon learned of the incident, described it, after extensive research, as likely the most interesting case in history. Betty Cash and Vickie Landrum sued the US government because of their cases of cancer, demanding compensation of $20 million. But the case turned out to be complex and difficult. The evidence Betty Cash and Vickie Landrum

Three years after the UFO episode, Betty Cash and Vickie Landrum developed cancer; according to their statements, this was due to the high dose of radiation when they encountered the UFO. The story became a national media event. The two women sued the US government for compensation in the amount of $20 million, but couldn't produce the necessary evidence.

The CH-47 is used by the US Army and Marines as a transport and rescue helicopter. Was the UFO escorted by a fleet of CH-47s because it was in danger of crashing? Testimony from witnesses is contradictory. (USAF)

were able to present to the court was based solely on the medical examination report and on the sightings of military helicopters, which made the eyewitnesses suspect that the military must have had something to do with the matter. But Betty Cash and Vickie Landrum stood empty-handed before the court during the main trial. They had no evidence in the form of photographs or videos to substantiate their suspicions. Betty Cash told the court that it was a large type of helicopter, a transport helicopter with two rotors. This may have been a CH-47 Chinook helicopter, which is used by the US Army and Marines as a transport and rescue helicopter, among other uses. Was there possibly a secret US Armed Forces test aircraft in the air that was in danger of crashing at the time in question? According

to witnesses, the object did indeed seem to have been out of control at times; was it in danger of crashing and did the helicopter squadron belong to a rescue team that would have had to immediately recover the object in case of a crash? A quite conceivable option, but the necessary evidence was lacking in court. Up until today, the entire incident has not been cleared up, and the clues led, as might be expected, to nothing. A nearby Air Force base, where CH-47 type helicopters were stationed at the time of the incident, responded to a written request that none of their helicopters had been in the air at the time in question. The responsible press officer, Major Tony Geisha, based in Fort Hood, also insisted that he knew nothing of any military operations at the given time. But the well-known lawyer Peter Gersten, representing Betty Cash and Vickie Landrum in court, did not give up and found more witnesses with the help of a detective. These included Lamar Walker of the Dayton Police Department. Walker and his wife together saw the helicopter fleet, but not the diamond-shaped object, as he testified in court. Another eyewitness was an employee of a nearby oil refinery, who had indeed seen the mysterious UFO during his night shift; at first he took this to be the tire manufacturer Goodyear advertising blimp. He didn't see the helicopter, so he also was soon dismissed as a credible witness from the court.

Only a year later did there seem to be a turning point in the case. A nearby military base held an open house, which Vickie Landrum visited together with her grandson Colby. There were CH-47 helicopters among the exhibits there, the type of helicopter that the three claimed they had seen accompanying the UFO on the night in question. Vickie Landrum immediately got palpitations when she saw the helicopter, and Colby at first found the sight scary, but both overcame their fear and soon even began to talk to one of the pilots. The pilot told them a lot about his work, and in this context, mentioned quite casually that he and others in a formation of twenty-two helicopters had to escort a UFO that was threatening to crash. The images of that night in question immediately came clearly into Vickie Landrum's mind, and she told the pilot that she and her grandson had been eyewitnesses to this incident. It apparently became clear to the pilot at this moment that he had probably gone a little too far in what he had said, and that he had betrayed secrets that could have far-reaching consequences for him. When Vickie Landrum asked the pilot anyway if he would reaffirm his testimony in court, he

reacted angrily and asked Vickie Landrum and her grandson to leave. Yet Vickie Landrum knew at that moment that what she, her grandson, and her friend, Betty, had experienced that evening, had been real, but they could not do much with the pilot's statement if he wasn't ready to make a statement before the court. Also in response to further inquiries from lawyers, the pilot denied he had ever said any such thing. Even more—he now claimed that Vickie Landrum had just imagined everything. The US government continued to deny any responsibility, and the court soon afterward ended the proceedings.

On May 22, 1982, a similar sighting again occurred: While patrolling near Cleveland, in Texas, Deputy Sheriff John McDonald saw an object that he described as a "diamond" to the *MUFON Journal*, colored gray and grimy, like galvanized steel. The object was large with red flashing lights and two white headlights. But in this case also, it was impossible to clarify the origin of the object, and the investigations produced no results. Again and again, eyewitnesses have reported in the past about mental and physical damage that they suffered due to close contact with a UFO. Subsequent investigations carried out on site in many cases revealed real anomalies in the soil and plants, which, therefore, proved that something actually must have happened. Thus, at around 7:00 p.m. on November 2, 1971, the sixteen-year-old son of a farmer from Delphos, in Kansas, saw an almost ten foot (three meter) wide, mushroom-shaped object approximately eighty-two feet (twenty-five meters) away, that hovered around two feet (sixty cm) above the ground in a wooded area. The object glowed alternately in the colors blue, red, and orange; he saw a bright zone of light between forest floor and the object and heard a sound that reminded him of the vibration of an old

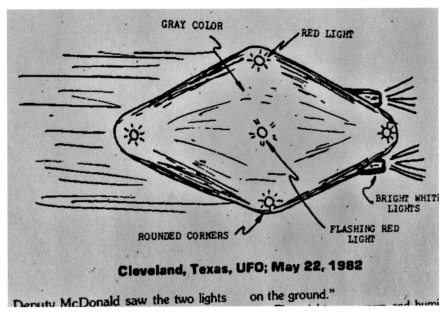

GRAY COLOR

RED LIGHT

BRIGHT WHIT LIGHTS

FLASHING RED LIGHT

ROUNDED CORNERS

Cleveland, Texas, UFO; May 22, 1982

Deputy McDonald saw the two lights on the ground."

On May 22, 1982, Deputy Sheriff John McDonald, on patrol near Cleveland, saw an object similar to that seen by Betty Cash and Vickie Landrum. (MUFON CES)

washing machine. The strange object took off after about five minutes and flew away. Afterward, the boy complained of burning eyes and severe headaches. Some hours after the object had flown away, the place over which the object had hovered began to glow. When the boy touched the ground, it hurt his fingertips and they felt numb for days—as if they had come into contact with dry ice. Subsequent soil samples from this place showed that the ground was water-repellent, and it was found to be chemiluminescent, for which no logical explanation could be found; only that the form of energy responsible for this was apparently not electromagnetic in nature.

Epilogue

There are many authentic photos of UFOs whose validity is always being doubted by skeptics. Already, in 1978, there were twenty-one rolls of film showing pictures of UFOs. Six of these rolls of film alone come from CIA sources. Some thirty-four images were classified as genuine by the Ground Saucer Watch photo analysis group in Phoenix, Arizona, which said that there is no conventional explanation for the images. The objects shown in the photographs are unknown ones. That such cases are completely inexplicable may be a reason that few scientists dare to seriously address the topic of UFOs or to speak of openly confronting the issue, although many senior figures (such as officers of the Russian and Belgian Armed Forces and the former defense minister of France, Robert Galley) have more than once expressed the view that the existence of UFOs is, in principle, possible. In 1978, Eric Gairy, the former Prime Minister of Grenada, even challenged the United Nations to investigate the issue of UFOs in more detail, but this kind of effort always comes to nothing, and it is, of course, not surprising that skeptics are taken more seriously than quite serious UFO researchers, who argue that the UFO phenomenon is real and it is really possible that we are not the only living beings in the universe. Recall that in the Middle Ages, people believed in the approximately 1,500-year-old world view of the Greek Ptolemy, that the Earth was the center of the universe, and all the other planets revolved around it. The astronomer Nicolaus Copernicus, born in 1473 in Torun, Poland, sought for evidence that, not the Earth, but the sun, was at the center of the planetary system. For a long time, the astronomer feared that other scholars would pour scorn on his research and that it could be rejected by the Church and, as a result, only informed a very few people from his close circle about his pioneering studies on the solar system. It was the famous scientist Galileo Galilei (1564–1642) who first took up Copernicus' research and provided the world with the physical proof of the Earth's orbital motion. Galileo also believed he would be able to convince the Church, but he was wrong in that view. His doctrine of the Earth's movement was declared absurd by the Church and termed blasphemy. Galileo was forced to recant his beliefs and was placed under arrest for life. Galileo was rehabilitated by the Vatican only in 1992. Are we now perhaps moving along a path similar to that of Galileo, more than 500 years ago, if we still claim that we are alone in the universe?

Take the example of Roswell. Up to today, official bodies have still not confirmed that an unknown flying object did indeed crash there, but on this point, we think about the numerous testimonies under oath. Witnesses, who saw something. Something that clearly could not have come from earth. Witnesses, some of whom were over eighty years old when they wanted to tell the world, under oath, that they had seen something that cannot be explained by conventional means. We must be allowed to pose the question: Why should all these people lie? Colonel Halt of Woodbridge Air Force base testified that what had landed in Rendlesham Forest, in 1980, clearly did not come from the Earth, and he also said later in an interview, that humanity is not yet ready to know the whole truth. It is clear that in the past, there have been more questions than answers on the subject. Questions that need to be addressed in the future. Perhaps mankind is thus standing on the threshold of a new era. Just as more than 500 years ago people couldn't believe that Earth was a sphere, perhaps

The astronomer Nicolaus Copernicus sought evidence that, not the Earth, but the sun, was at the center of the planetary system.

Galileo Galilei (1564–1642) first took up Copernicus' research and provided the world with the physical proof of the Earth's orbital motion.

today, we simply cannot really imagine that it is quite possible that there is more life in the universe. Civilizations that are perhaps many times superior to us in evolutionary terms. This book is intended to suggest that perhaps we should put our firmly established world view into question and at least not exclude the possibility that there is more between heaven and Earth than we believe we know today.

Is it likely that we are alone in the universe? Or do civilizations exist that are perhaps far superior to us and, therefore, are able to visit far distant planetary systems? (NASA)

Bibliography

UFOs over Germany

Darmstadt-based newspaper. "Messel was visited by aliens at night?" 03/16/1982, *Abendpost: "Darmstadt im UFO Fieber,"* 03/17/1982.

Kirstein, Dennis. "The lights of Greifswald-UFO mystery vs. IFO solution." www.ufoinformation.de.

Ludwiger, Illobrand von. *The State of UFO Research. Verlag of Zweitausendeins,* 1992 (Central Investigation Committee on Aerial Phenomena [CENAP].

Zweites Deutsches Fernsehen. "Hub." 03/16/1982.

And They Came in Fiery Chariots

Hesemann, Michael. *Classified UFO.* Germany: Bechtermünz Verlag, 1998.

Jung, Carl Gustav. *A Modern Myth of Things Seen in the Sky.* Germany: Rascher Verlag, 1958.

Thompson, Keith. *Angels and Aliens.* Germany: Knaur, 1993.

Searching for Traces

Arnold, Kenneth. "I Did See the Flying Disks." *Fate Magazine* Volume 1." Spring 1948.

Die Welt: "The Theory of the Mysterious UFO over Bremen." 01/07/2014.

Die Welt: "UFO Ensures Flight Cancellations at Bremen Airport." 01/07/2014.

Hynek, J. Allen. *UFO Encounters of the First, Second and Third Kind.* Goldmann, 1978.

Ruppelt, Edward E. "The Report on Unidentified Flying Objects." New York, 1958.

FBI: Project Blue Book Report

Central Investigation Committee on Aerial Phenomena (CENAP). "Russian UFO anniversary: Petrozavodsk, the Sky Jellyfish. " *CENAP News,* 2007.

Discovery Communications, Inc. "UFO—Uncovering the Evidence." 1996.

Fiebag, Johannes. *The UFO Syndrome,* Germany: Knaur, 1996.

Good, Timothy. *Need to Know—UFOs, the Military, and Intelligence,* Berkeley, CA: Pegasus Books, 2007.

Holbe, Rainer. "Fantastic Phenomena." Germany: Herbig, 1993.

Haines, Richard F. "Aviation Safety in America—A Previously Neglected Factor." National Aviation Reporting Center on Anomalous Phenomena (NARCAP) Report, 2000.

Kean, Leslie. *"UFOs Generals, Pilots and Government Officials Break Silence."* Germany: Koppe Verlag, 2012.

Klass, Philip J. "FAA Data Sheds New Light on JAL Pilot's UFO Report." *The Skeptical Inquirer* 12 No. 1, Buffalo NY, 1987.

Maccabee, Bruce. "The Fantastic Flight of JAL 1628." *International UFO Reporter,* 2011.

Personal interviews with eyewitnesses.

UFOs Over the Soviet Union

Ludwiger, Illobrand von. *The State of UFO Research.* Germany: Verlag Zweitausendeins, 1992.

UFO Sightings by Pilots

Steucke, Paul. "Office of Public Affairs, Alaskan Region, Federal Aviation Administration, Department of Transport: FAA Releases Documents on Reported UFO Sighting Last November." Anchorage, 1987

The Roswell File

Berlitz, Charles & William Moore L. *The Roswell Zwischenfall—the UFOs and the CIA.* Germany: Knaur, 1980.

Bruni, Georgina. *You Can't Tell the People: The Definitive Account of the Rendlesham Forest UFO Mystery.* United Kingdom: Sidgwick & Jackson, 2001.

Buttlar, Johannes von. *The Aliens from Roswell Protocol of a Conspiracy.* Germany: Lübbe, 1996.

Daily Mail. "It was a craft that did not come from this planet: CIA agent speaks out on 65th anniversary of Roswell UFO landings." 2012.

Kean, Leslie. *UFOs Generals, Pilots and Government Officials Break Silence.* Germany: Koppe Verlag, 2012.

Ludwiger, Illobrand von. *UFOs—The Unwanted Truth.* Germany: Kopp Verlag, 2009.

Penniston speech at the National Press Club in Washington, DC, 2007.

Schmitt, Cary and Donald. *Witness to Roswell,* New Jersey: Career Press, 2009.

The Secret of the Black Triangles

Belgian Society for the Study of Space Phenomena (SOBEPS). *UFO Wave over Belgium,* Verlag Zweitausendeins, 1994.

Central Investigation Committee on Aerial Phenomena (CENAP): Belgium. "A Sky Full of Easter UFOs."

Hesemann, Michael. *Classified UFO.* Germany: Bechtermünz Verlag, 1998.

Ludwiger, Illobrand von. *The State of UFO research.* Germany: Verlag Zweitausendeins, 1992.

Leclet, Renaud. "The Belgium UFO Wave of 1989–1992." pdf.

Ledoux, Samuel and Joselin Fedunspi. "Mea culpa de l'auteur de la photo d'ovni truqueé de Petit Rechain." *Le Journal*—Le 19 Heures, RTLTV1 (Belgium), 2011.

The Telegraph. "UFO Files: Belgian fighters scrambled to investigate UFOs." 2009.

Area 51—America's Secret World

Der Tagesspiegel. "Conspiracy theories—CIA confirms existence of mysterious area 51." 2013.

The Independent. "The (very) secret history of Area 51." 2011

ORF Austrian TV. "The Secret of Area 51." 2011.

Rothschild Fouche, Edgar. *Alien Rapture: The Chosen.* MN: Galde Press, 1998.

The Case of Betty Cash & Vickie Landrum

CUFON.org: "Transcript of Bergstrom AFB Interview of Betty Cash, Vickie & Colby Landrum." Part 1 of 2, 2012.

Klass, Philip J. "CSI The Skeptics." *UFO Newsletter* Volume 56, 1999.

Ludwiger, Illobrand von. *The State of UFO Research.* Germany: Zweitausendeins, 1992.

ufocasebook. "The Piney Woods Incident, Cash Landrum." 1998.

About the Author

FRANK SCHWEDE has been a journalist for more than thirty years and has documented numerous UFO sightings, spoken to eyewitnesses, and has been able to come to the conclusion that ninety-nine percent of the witnesses he spoke to were credible. His goal is to get on the track of the truth, or at least get closer to it.